"Sit & Get"
Won't Grow Dendrites

SECOND EDITION

Marcia L. Tate

"Sit & Get"
Won't Grow Dendrites

SECOND EDITION

20
Professional
Learning Strategies
That Engage
the Adult Brain

CORWIN
A SAGE Company

CORWIN
A SAGE Company

FOR INFORMATION:

Corwin

A SAGE Company

2455 Teller Road

Thousand Oaks, California 91320

(800) 233-9936

www.corwin.com

SAGE Publications Ltd.

1 Oliver's Yard

55 City Road

London EC1Y 1SP

United Kingdom

SAGE Publications India Pvt. Ltd.

B 1/I 1 Mohan Cooperative Industrial Area

Mathura Road, New Delhi 110 044

India

SAGE Publications Asia-Pacific Pte. Ltd.

3 Church Street

#10-04 Samsung Hub

Singapore 049483

Acquisitions Editor: Carol Chambers Collins

Senior Associate Editor: Megan Bedell

Senior Editorial Assistant: Sarah Bartlett

Senior Permissions Editor: Jason Kelley

Project Editor: Veronica Stapleton

Copy Editor: Kim Husband

Typesetter: C&M Digitals (P) Ltd.

Proofreader: Barbara Johnson

Indexer: Marilyn Augst

Front Cover Designer: Anthony Paular

Back Cover Designer: Rose Storey

Copyright © 2012 by Corwin

Printed in the United States of America

Library of Congress Cataloging-in-Publication Data

Tate, Marcia L.

"Sit & get" won't grow dendrites : 20 professional learning strategies that engage the adult brain / Marcia L. Tate.— 2nd ed.

p. cm.

Includes bibliographical references and index.

ISBN 978-1-4129-9934-2 (pbk. : alk. paper)

1. Adult learning. 2. Teachers—In-service training. I. Title.

LC5225.L42T37 2012

374—dc23   2012011686

This book is printed on acid-free paper.

SUSTAINABLE FORESTRY INITIATIVE
Certified Chain of Custody
Promoting Sustainable Forestry
www.sfiprogram.org
SFI-01268

SFI label applies to text stock

14 15 16 17 18 10 9 8 7 6 5 4 3 2

Contents

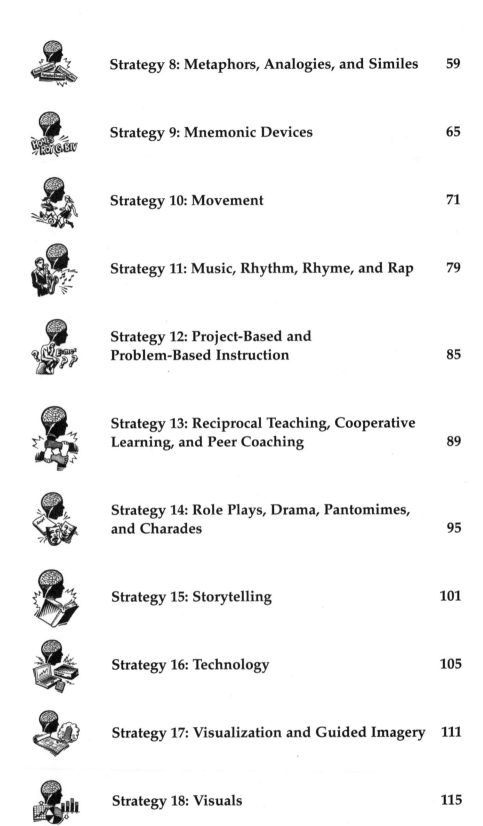

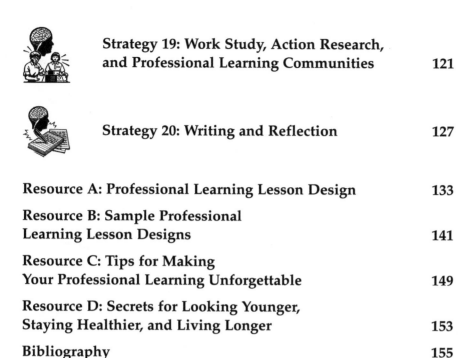

Preface

When I teach the course by the same name as this book, one of the first activities in which I engage my participants is to have them visualize the best or the worst presentation they have been a part of as an adult learner and then share the experience with a partner. Several participants then volunteer to share their stories with the entire class, enabling me to hear some amazing bad and good examples regarding teaching the adult learner. Here are just a few of the more memorable quotes.

WORST ■

My presenter showed us multiple PowerPoint slides and then read the PowerPoint to us as if we could not read ourselves!

I attended a conference on the brain at a prestigious university where they shared the research about the positive effects of movement on the brain and body. In three days, we never moved once!

My workshop leader read from his prepared notes in a monotone voice, never lifting his eyes from the paper or engaging us in any way.

My presenter became ill during the presentation and, instead of cancelling the workshop, she laid prone on the floor and scrolled through her PowerPoint slides with her clicker while simultaneously explaining each slide to us, from her position on the floor no less!

The teacher became upset because a student disagreed with a statement he made. He began to argue with the student while the remainder of the class just watched!

I am pretty sure there must be PowerPoint in hell!

Our principal asks for the faculty's input and then does precisely what she was going to do anyway. We never feel as if we have a voice.

My graduate professor sat in a chair and read from his notes what he wanted us to know. The pages of the notes were so yellow that I am sure he had been using these same notes for years.

My principal used a faculty meeting to berate the entire faculty because our test scores did not increase this year. We all felt so dejected that we didn't even want to teach the next day!

All we ever did while I was working on my master's degree was read books and write papers, read books and write papers, read books and write papers. I don't remember anything I learned that I could actually use to improve instruction for my second graders.

■ BEST

I have attended staff development inservices for all my professional life. I still remember the one time the presenter was at the door to greet me.

The presenter kept my attention the entire time with his personal stories. I still remember some of the emotional ones and the concepts he taught us as he told the stories.

My presenter was hilarious! He had a natural sense of humor that permeated the entire presentation and kept us laughing the entire time.

Following the presentation, I could immediately apply so much of what I learned during the presentation.

Our school is a professional learning community so that every opportunity to meet together as a faculty has an express purpose. It has brought the staff closer together.

My graduate professor assigned projects which I could immediately try out with my third grade class. I learned so much that year!

It was 7:30 p.m. and time for the workshop to end and, even though I worked all day, I was still energized. I remember thinking, Is it time to go already?

I learned as much from the participants in my class as we talked together as I did from my teacher.

My best learning as an adult actually came from my peer coach, who had the patience, wisdom, and knowledge to help me achieve the goals that we had set together.

There was something for everyone in the presentation regardless of how you learned best!

■ 20 STRATEGIES FOR TEACHING THE ADULT BRAIN

In nearly all professions, adults are required to attend meetings, workshops, and classes during which pertinent content is imparted. Professional developers, consultants, administrators, college and university professors, and even keynote speakers who have the privilege of teaching adults are obligated to make their presentations memorable. Yet, all too often, they do not. How many times have you sat through a staff meeting, workshop, or even a semester-long course and left asking, *What did he say?* or *What did I actually learn?* How many times did you cram for an exam only to forget the information just as soon as the exam had ended?

Let me tell you a true story. Last summer, I was sitting in the lobby of the Hampton Inn in Dallas, Texas, eating breakfast when I overheard a conversation between two executives for a sales company sitting at a nearby table. One was going to present to the sales staff that day and was discussing his presentation with a coworker. He related that he had been told to limit the presentation so he had whittled it down to 100 PowerPoint slides. I bowed my head in prayer! Not for him—for his audience! Then he went on to say that each slide would take approximately 3 minutes of explanation. Can you imagine an audience listening to and looking at 300 minutes of PowerPoint? I call that *Death by PowerPoint!*

Close to 40 years in this profession have taught me that there are instructional strategies that can teach anybody anything because, by their very nature, these strategies take advantage of ways in which the brain learns best. Although these strategies are used most often in kindergarten or with primary grade students, with minor modifications, they work similarly for adult brains as well. After all, you do remember the book *All I Really Need to Know I Learned in Kindergarten*! Speakers and teachers who use these strategies are remembered because they have participants who are capable of understanding and retaining large amounts of information. On a more personal note, for many years I have received extremely positive evaluations of my presentations to adult audiences. I now realize that those evaluations are due in large part to the consistent use of the 20 brain-compatible strategies outlined in this book. You will find them applicable not only to what happens during the presentation of new information to adult audiences but also during other professional learning activities that are so crucial for long-term retention and behavior change.

WHY THESE STRATEGIES? ■

Theories abound from researchers such as Howard Gardner (1983), Robert Sternberg (1997), Sternberg and Grigorenko, (2000), and Bernice McCarthy (1990) related to the variety of ways that individuals acquire and retain content. An exciting sign of our time is the fact that brain research now provides neurological rationales as to why some strategies simply work best, not only for student brains but for adult brains as well. Consultants like Eric Jensen (2008, 2009a, 2009b), David Sousa (2006), and Patricia Wolfe (2001) continue to make practical application for educators from this important research. Yet the very strategies that are recommended for teachers to use in instructing students are seldom modeled during presentations to adult audiences. For this reason, many teachers abhor staff development workshops and courses and actually bring other things to do while their boring presenter is teaching.

It doesn't have to be that way. Nor should it! While I was teaching in Australia, a chemistry teacher walked up to me at the first break and pulled a complicated crossword puzzle from his pocket. He told me that he had actually planned to complete the puzzle discretely during the course of my workshop. He admitted that he had not taken the crossword from his pocket until that moment since I had kept him so engaged throughout the entire morning. He thanked me for that. I thank the 20 strategies!

After perusing both learning style and brain research, I have identified 20 strategies that take advantage of the ways all of our brains learn best—adults as well as young people. Because these strategies support both learning style theory and brain research, they enable all teachers to plan and deliver powerful, memorable presentations that have the potential to change adults' minds in light of new information. (See Figure Intro 1 for a comparison of these 20 strategies to learning theories, such as the multiple intelligences and visual, auditory, tactile, and kinesthetic modalities.)

Those who facilitate professional learning have come to believe that no matter how meaningful the initial learning, it is what happens within the context of the job that matters most. Hord (2009), Joyce and Calhoun (2010), and Knight (2009) tell us that it is the job-embedded practice and the follow-up and support that most often lead to sustained improvements in professional practice for the majority of educators Therefore, this book also highlights professional learning activities such as peer coaching, action research, project-based instruction, and teacher-led study groups, all embedded under the umbrella of professional learning communities. This turns fragmented professional learning into meaningful opportunities for growth, resulting in changes in practice and, ultimately, increased student achievement.

The book you are about to read attempts to accomplish the following six objectives:

- Offer an overview of some of the ways adult learners differ from their younger counterparts
- Identify and describe each of the 20 brain-compatible strategies as they relate to adult learning theory
- Provide a theoretical framework as to why these strategies appear to take advantage of the way adult brains acquire and retain information best
- Supply more than 150 professional learning activities during which these instructional strategies can be used to ensure that adults are acquiring the knowledge, skills, and attitudes necessary for improving their practice
- Equip the reader with opportunities to reflect on and apply these strategies either during or following a meeting, workshop, course, or any other professional learning activity
- Delineate several sample lesson plans that can serve as models for the reader to develop exemplary faculty meetings, workshops, or courses with appropriate follow-up

The activities in this book are merely a sampling of what is possible when professional developers, administrators, college professors, or anyone who teaches adults develops and delivers lessons that incorporate brain-compatible strategies. Once you begin to figure out which strategy is most appropriate for accomplishing a faculty meeting or course objectives, you will be capable of creating lessons easily. This is why the last section in each chapter asks you to reflect on the application of the strategy for your own specific meeting, workshop, or follow-up.

Wouldn't it make sense for those who facilitate professional learning for adults to model the same strategies and practices during the learning opportunity that they would expect their participants to use with their own students? It has been said, *If you are not modeling what you are teaching, then you are teaching something else!* In fact, I am honored to say that a professional learning department in Ontario, California, has turned my last name into a verb. Prior to delivering a presentation, they asked one another the following question, *Have you Tated your presentation?* Another way to ask the same question: *Have you incorporated the 20 strategies into your presentation?*

You will begin to realize that you are doing something right when what has happened to me happens to you. Picture this: It is eight o'clock at night, and you tell your participants that class is over. The following question resounds: *Do we really have to go home?* However, you will really know that your professional learning experience has made a lasting difference when teachers tell you of their improved practice and the increases in their students' achievement. After all, isn't that what matters most?

Comparison of Professional Learning Strategies to Learning Theory		
Professional Learning Strategies	*Multiple Intelligences*	*Learning Modality*
Brainstorming and discussion	Verbal-linguistic	Auditory
Drawing and artwork	Spatial	Kinesthetic/tactile
Field trips	Naturalist	Kinesthetic/tactile
Games	Interpersonal	Kinesthetic/tactile
Graphic organizers, semantic maps, and word webs	Logical-mathematical/ spatial	Visual/tactile
Humor and celebration	Verbal-linguistic	Auditory
Manipulatives and models	Logical-mathematical	Tactile
Metaphors, analogies, and similes	Spatial	Visual/auditory
Mnemonic devices	Musical-rhythmic	Visual/auditory
Movement	Bodily-kinesthetic	Kinesthetic
Music, rhythm, rhyme, and rap	Musical-rhythmic	Auditory
Project-based and problem-based instruction	Logical-mathematical	Visual/tactile
Reciprocal teaching, cooperative learning, and peer coaching	Verbal-linguistic	Auditory
Role plays, drama, pantomimes, and charades	Bodily-kinesthetic	Kinesthetic
Storytelling	Verbal-linguistic	Auditory
Technology	Spatial	Visual/tactile
Visualization and guided imagery	Spatial	Visual
Visuals	Spatial	Visual
Work study, action research, and professional learning communities	Interpersonal	Kinesthetic
Writing and reflection	Interpersonal	Visual/tactile

Figure Intro 1

Acknowledgments

Have you ever been to a professional learning opportunity at which the primary emphasis is student engagement, only to be talked at for most of the day by the presenter? One of my participants related to me that she spent several days at a very prestigious university learning about the effects of movement and engagement on the brain. She stated that in those several days of instruction, the participants never moved once unless it was time for breaks or lunch.

For more than 25 years, I have presented to adult audiences. This book is dedicated to those people who teach adults while practicing what they preach by realizing that their participants are just as bored looking at a plethora of PowerPoint slides as are their younger counterparts in school.

I also acknowledge the educational consultants, like Eric Jensen, David Sousa, Robert Sylwester, and Patricia Wolfe, who continue to convey how the student and adult brain should be taught. These experts on the brain show us that having people sit and get information is not the way to grow dendrites, or brain cells, and that concepts are remembered longer if they are taught in ways that are compatible with how the brain actually acquires and retains information.

I also acknowledge those schools and school systems in which professional learning is not a one-shot workshop but in which teachers are working in professional learning communities, looking at student achievement data and increasing their own learning and that of their students while making definitive plans to accomplish school and school system goals and objectives.

It was my husband, Tyrone, who first encouraged me to expand my teaching abilities to those of adult audiences. For that, I will be forever grateful! My children—Jennifer and her husband Lex, Jessica, and Christopher and his wife Amanda—have followed me

xvii

for years as I have dragged them to workshops taught all over the country. I am grateful for their continued support!

I am especially thankful to our administrative assistants, Carol Purviance and Fran Rodrigues, and the associates who continue to make the company, *Developing Minds Inc.*, thrive. One of those associates is my daughter, Jennifer, who has followed in my footsteps, as she also teaches adults. Thank you, Carol Collins, my editor, for your continued advice, support, and encouragement. You are truly appreciated!

About the Author

Marcia L. Tate, Ed.D., is the former executive director of professional development for the DeKalb County School System, Decatur, Georgia, and has been presenting to adult audiences for more than 25 years. During her 30-year career with the school district, she has been a classroom teacher, reading specialist, language arts coordinator, and staff development executive director. She received the Distinguished Staff Development Award for the State of Georgia, and her department was chosen to receive the Exemplary Program Award for the state.

Marcia is currently an educational consultant and has taught more than 350,000 administrators, teachers, parents, and business and community leaders throughout the world, including Australia, Egypt, Hungary, Singapore, Thailand, New Zealand, Oman, and Greece. She is the author of the following five bestsellers: *Worksheets Don't Grow Dendrites: 20 Instructional Strategies That Engage the Brain;* *"Sit & Get" Won't Grow Dendrites: 20 Professional Learning Strategies That Engage the Adult Brain; Reading and Language Arts Worksheets Don't Grow Dendrites: 20 Literacy Strategies That Engage the Brain; Shouting Won't Grow Dendrites: 20 Techniques for Managing a Brain-compatible Classroom;* and *Mathematics Worksheets Don't Grow Dendrites: 20 Numeracy Strategies That Engage the Brain,* as well as the texts, *Science Worksheets Don't Grow Dendrites: 20 Instructional Strategies That Engage the Brain,* and *Social Studies Worksheets Don't Grow Dendrites: 20 Instructional Strategies That Engage the Brain.* She is also the author of a popular book for parents called *Preparing Children for Success in School and in Life: 20 Ways to Increase Your Child's Brain Power.* Participants in her workshops refer to them as "some of the best ones they have ever experienced," since Marcia uses the 20 strategies outlined in her books to actively engage her audiences.

Marcia received her bachelor's degree in psychology and elementary education from Spelman College in Atlanta, Georgia. She earned her master's degree in remedial reading from the University of Michigan, her specialist degree in educational leadership from Georgia State University, and her doctorate in educational leadership from Clark Atlanta University. Spelman College awarded her the Apple Award for excellence in the field of education.

Marcia is married to Tyrone Tate and is the proud mother of three children—Jennifer, Jessica, and Christopher—and the doting grandmother of two granddaughters, Christian and Aidan, and one grandson, Maxwell. Marcia can be contacted by calling her company at (770) 918–5039 or by e-mail: marciata@bellsouth.net. Visit her website atwww.developingmindsinc.com.

Introduction

Adult Learning Theory

Fold your arms. Look down and see whether your right arm is crossed over your left or vice versa. Now, reverse the process. If your right arm was crossed over your left, cross your left over your right.

You have just experienced change. How did it feel? *Awkward, unnatural, weird,* and *uncomfortable* are just a few of the adjectives people use to describe their feelings following the completion of this activity in my workshop on teaching the adult brain. These are also some of the same adjectives that teachers and administrators use when describing their reactions to new behaviors or skills they are being asked to implement—*awkward, unnatural, weird,* and *uncomfortable.* In fact, some people are so resistant to change that when coronary bypass patients were asked to choose between an increased risk of dying and the lifestyle change they will have to make, 90% would not make the change (Deutschman, 2005). It has even been said that the only one who truly likes change is a wet baby.

Change is inevitable. In fact, the only way to improve the status quo is to change it. However, there seems to be an order to this thing called change. In his book, *Evaluating Professional Development,* (Guskey, 1999) relates that when changes need to be made, there are three variables to consider. They are as follows:

- teacher attitudes
- student outcomes
- teacher behaviors

Now before I reveal the appropriate order, answer this question: Which one of the three aforementioned variables should change first, which second, and which third? When I pose that

"Some of the ideas in the staff development meeting on innovation seemed interesting but they've never been tried before so I think I'll hold off for now."

question to my audience, most people say that **teacher attitudes** should change first. Is that what you said? According to Guskey, it is **teacher behavior** that should change first. After all, as an administrator, I cannot change a teacher's attitude. A teacher must change his or her own attitude. I can only create the conditions under which teachers will change behavior, or do some things differently. As the behaviors change, **student outcomes** change. Students begin to score higher on tests, discipline problems decrease, and/ or teaching and learning become fun. Eventually, over time, **teacher attitudes** also change. Let's examine the e-mail below that I received from a teacher who attended one of my workshops. Guskey's order of change is actually reflected in her e-mail.

Hi Dr. Tate,

I attended your workshop while you were in Spartanburg. I went home that weekend and planned a week of lessons that instilled the 20 strategies and tried them out on my first and fourth period biology classes. **(behavior change)** *WOW! What a different class! I am so jazzed—I have heard comments amongst the students such as "I feel so smart in this class." "I have never been good at science, now I am making A's!"* **(student outcome change)** *This is enough to fuel me to keep working hard to plan great lessons that hook my students in.* **[attitude change]**

> *Michelle Arena,*
> *Chemistry/Biology Teacher*
> *Boiling Springs High School*
> *Boiling Springs, SC*

Let's consider some of the conditions under which the adult brain learns best.

ADULTS LEARN BEST WHEN . . . ■

They Have Input Into the Selection of the Content and Even Development of the Learning Experiences (Hord, 2009; Sparks, 2009)

Throughout my 40 years in education, I have worked with many frustrated teachers inundated with mandates being thrust on them by the forces beyond their control, such as federal and state departments of education, school system superintendents, and well-intentioned building principals. According to Dennis Sparks (2009), *telling* adults what to do or *forcing* them to do it are two common approaches used in schools that do not have the strength to continuously improve the practices of teachers.

In the early 1990s, theorists (Senge, 1990; Sergiovanni, 1992) revisited the notion that when people are directly involved in the systemic processes of an organization, they are more amenable to the changes that result from their involvement. They wrote about corporations and schools as *learning organizations* in which, rather than being told what professional development needed to occur, colleagues worked together to develop a shared vision and make that vision a reality. The professional development was then driven by what the data indicated.

This idea is also the basic premise of the *professional learning community.* In a professional learning community, members of that school or community "thoughtfully study multiple sources of student data to discover where students are performing well, and thus where staff members can celebrate" (Hord, 2009, p. 40). Hord (2009) delineates the following six dimensions of professional learning communities:

- Beliefs, values, and vision, shared by all members of the community of what the school should be
- Leadership, power, and decision-making shared and distributed among members of the community
- Structural conditions such as time, resources, and place supportive of the community's work
- Community members caring for, respecting, trusting, and supporting one another
- Members intentionally learning together while addressing student needs and the effectiveness of the members
- Peers improving individually and the organization improving as a whole through members sharing their practice and gaining feedback from one another

The Learning Is Connected to the Vast Background of Knowledge and Experience That the Adult Brings to the Table (Burns, Menchaca, & Dimock, 2001)

In my more than 25 years of teaching adults and 40 years of teaching students, I have found one major difference. Adults have simply lived longer, experienced more things, and gained more knowledge, wisdom, and understanding. According to Burns, Menchaca, and Dimock (2001), one principle that is crucial to constructivist learning theory is the learner bringing his or her unique experiences, beliefs, and knowledge to the learning situation. This makes the adult a valuable asset to the learning environment; however, it also makes a group of adult learners more heterogeneous than a group of younger students. For these reasons, adults prefer to take charge of their own learning and connect any new knowledge to what they already know.

Because adult learners have experienced so much, they place a higher priority on internal motivators (such as increased job satisfaction, higher self-esteem, improved instructional delivery) rather than external motivators. Therefore, asking adults their expectations for the course or having them give input into the development of lessons is a much more effective technique than providing them with longer breaks or an early dismissal time.

In my workshops, my participants and I learn as much from other participants as they do from me. Many of the 20 strategies outlined in this book provide opportunities for adults to share their rich personal experiences with their peers. By the time they have participated in whole-class and small-group discussion, retaught a concept to a close partner or a date, told an emotional story from their past to illustrate a point, or asked a question in the class *Parking Lot*, adults have shared their expertise to enhance the class content.

The Learning Is Both Received and Processed in More Than One Way (Gardner, 1983, 1999; Jensen, 2008, 2009a; Tate, 2010, 2011)

There is no shortage of learning style theories supporting multiple modalities. These theories include Howard Gardner's (1983, 1999) *Multiple Intelligences*, Bernice McCarthy's (1990) *4MAT Model*, and Robert Sternberg's (1997; Sternberg & Grigorenko, 2000) *Successful Intelligence*, as well as the theory that in any group of participants, there are at least four major modalities represented: *visual, auditory, kinesthetic*, and *tactile*.

Like the students they teach, adults also learn through multiple modalities. Whenever I teach a group of adult learners, I am cognizant of the fact that among the participants, there are those who simply must see what is being taught. These are my visual learners, and for them I utilize the document camera, flip charts, and video clips. (Refer to *Strategy 17: Visualization and Guided Imagery* and *Strategy 18: Visuals* for specific activities for visual learners.)

For auditory learners in my classes, participants select close partners and make dates at which they discuss content and work in cooperative groups or families. They engage in both whole-class and small-group discussion. (Refer to *Strategy 1: Brainstorming and Discussion* and *Strategy 13: Reciprocal Teaching, Cooperative Learning, and Peer Coaching* for specific activities that address the auditory modality.)

Then there are those participants who simply need hands-on experiences. These are the tactile learners who most enjoy the short writing experiences and the drawing, as well as the use of manipulatives during the learning experience. (Refer to *Strategy 2: Drawing and Artwork, Strategy 7: Manipulatives and Models*, and *Strategy 20: Writing and Reflection* for specific professional learning activities that address the tactile modality.)

Finally, it is usually the kinesthetic participants who are the most neglected and who find it difficult to wait for the scheduled breaks to move. This is why participants in my class dance the *number-line hustle*, role play specific concepts, and move to meet with *appointments* or *dates*. (Refer to *Strategy 10: Movement* and *Strategy 14: Role Plays, Drama, Pantomimes, and Charades* for specific activities geared for these learners.)

By the time the learning experience has ended, all four major modalities have been addressed and the needs of all adult learners met. More importantly, at the conclusion of any course, adults have multiple ways to recall content, in both the short and long term.

The Learning Is Collegial and Directed at Solving Specific Job-Related Problems (Dufour, 1991; Goodlad, 1984; Nolly, 2011)

Almost 30 years ago, John Goodlad (1984) informed us that teachers were so isolated in their respective classrooms that they were rarely provided with the opportunity to work with their colleagues for any reason, including solving specific schoolwide problems. Teaching has even been described as *the second most private act in which adults engage* (Dufour, 1991). Yet andragogy tells us that adults learn most effectively when engaged collaboratively with peers. This collaboration is key to professional learning as teachers apply new knowledge and skill and should include teachers of gifted, special-needs, and mainstreamed students. According to Nolly (2009), when teachers are confronting similar issues or problems and are encouraged to discuss those issues and share solutions, it promotes the sense that it is possible to improve.

However, functioning effectively in groups does not just happen. In fact, even the best of teams appear to go through the following four stages of development:

- *Forming.* During Stage 1, group members are spending time making sure their ideas will be respected, defining roles, determining group parameters, and often feeling threatened. During this stage, group members are most dependent on the leader, and the group may be least productive.
- *Storming.* In Stage 2, group members' needs begin to be met, and they experience a degree of influence and responsibility. This stage may be characterized by questions to authority, conflicts, or leadership struggles. However, it is a necessary stage in group development. As internal facilitator for the strategic planning process in my school district, I recall one action team that spent an inordinate amount of time in the storming stage. This group eventually became the most productive of all eight teams, however, and formulated the most effective action plans.
- *Norming.* By the time a group reaches Stage 3, it has begun to accept and even respect the differences of individual

members and to become dependent on them. Group members feel comfortable enough with one another to criticize constructively, share problems, and establish group norms.

- *Performing.* Stage 4 is the highest stage of the group process. By this time, group members are performing interdependently. Displays of affection are obvious. The leader is serving as facilitator and group members are engaged in effective problem solving.

Strategy 1: Brainstorming and Discussion, Strategy 12: Project-Based and Problem-Based Instruction, Strategy 13: Reciprocal Teaching, Cooperative Learning, and Peer Coaching, and *Strategy 19: Work Study, Action Research, and Professional Learning Communities* are replete with additional research on the advantages of utilizing the group process to problem solve and activities for involving participants in effective professional learning group activities.

They Have Ample Opportunity to Reflect on the Implementation of the New Competencies (Garmston & Wellman, 1999; Mezirow, 1991)

Garmston and Wellman (1999) stated that *"any group too busy to reflect about its work is too busy to improve"* (p. 63). In the absence of reflection, teachers either tend not to change behavior, or spend too much time simply recounting everything that has not worked in the past.

Adults have a difficult time separating their background of experiences from who they are personally. For this reason, Jack Mezirow (1991) suggested that adults engage in reflective learning that enables them to assess and reassess their personal assumptions.

I must admit that one of my personal goals is to provide more time in my professional learning for adults to reflect on an activity that just took place, since it is not the activity that is the most important aspect, it is the reflection on the activity. It is during this time that adults can consider how the activity compares with their personal beliefs and assumptions and discuss those assumptions with other learners. For example, in one class, we discuss why it is so difficult for adults to change their behavior. I get a group of participants to stand in a circle and toss a ball in the same order to the same person each time. When the group only has one ball, the tossing goes smoothly. Then I introduce a new ball, then another new ball, then another new ball. The group has to keep the throwing pattern going with four balls without dropping a single one. You can probably guess what happens. Balls start falling all over the place. I then give each group time to reflect on what this activity has to do with the responsibilities we place on teachers. This reflection is one of the most meaningful parts of the workshop.

Following Initial Training, Adults Are Provided With Ongoing Support That Can Take the Form of Peer Coaching or Study Groups (Joyce & Calhoun, 2010; Knight, 2009; Westwater & Wolfe, 2000)

Have you ever heard of the term *pigeon staff development?* This term is often used to describe inservices or workshops at which a consultant from outside the school system *flies in, drops a load, and then flies off.* Don't visualize that! It is not pretty! Experience has informed us that this type of professional learning rarely results in sustained improvement in practice. Brain research is confirming what staff developers have always known—that learning must be linked to real-life experiences for the learner to retain and later apply what is being learned (Westwater & Wolfe, 2000).

One of the most effective forms of follow-up is fulfilled by the role of the coach. Whether they are referred to as academic coaches, cognitive coaches, literacy coaches, or math coaches, this crucial role improves a school's ability to educate its students by enhancing the way teachers teach (Knight, 2009). Eight commonalities of the coaching position are as follows:

- The major focus is on a teacher's professional practice.
- The coach's experiences with the teacher relate directly to lessons taught in the teacher's classroom.
- The coaching is intense and may continue over days, weeks, or months.
- Coaches are partners with teachers, who have some control over the meetings.
- Coaches engage in dialogue with teachers in which the conversation is reflective.
- Coaches are not evaluators and should not make judgmental decisions regarding the teachers.
- Teachers can talk with coaches confidentially without fear of their conversations being shared with others.
- Coaches should be great communicators, listeners, questioners, and observers whose feedback should be encouraging, energizing, honest, and practical (Knight, 2009).

Learning Forward, formerly the National Staff Development Council, has developed the following national standards that serve to undergird the content, context, and process of all professional learning opportunities.

STANDARDS FOR PROFESSIONAL ■
LEARNING (LEARNING FORWARD, 2011)

Professional Learning That Increases Educator Effectiveness and Results for All Students

Learning Communities

- Occurs within learning communities committed to continuous improvement, collective responsibility, and goal alignment;

Leadership

- Requires skillful leaders who develop capacity, advocate, and create support systems for professional learning;

Resources

- Requires prioritizing, monitoring, and coordinating resources for educator learning;

Data

- Uses a variety of sources and types of student, educator, and system data to plan, assess, and evaluate professional learning;

Learning Designs

- Integrates theories, research, and models of human learning to achieve its intended outcomes;

Implementation

- Applies research on change and sustains support for implementation of professional learning for long-term change;

Outcomes

- Aligns its outcome with educator performance and student curriculum standards.

It has always been the teacher who has made the difference. Therefore, anything that can be done to improve the effectiveness of the teacher is time well spent! When I taught in Singapore, I discovered that teachers there spend approximately 100 hours per year in professional development exploits. The same is true for Finland and South Korea. Why can't we take a lesson from our counterparts in other countries? I believe that my favorite quote says it best:

> *Teachers are those who use themselves as bridges over which they invite their students to cross; then, having facilitated their crossing, they joyfully collapse, inviting their students to build bridges of their own.*

This book will enable you to assist teachers in building better and stronger bridges that can lead students to improve academic achievement and love of learning.

Strategy 1

Brainstorming and Discussion

WHAT: DEFINING THE STRATEGY

What is it we want our students to know and be able to do as a result of this course or unit of instruction?

How will we know when each student has learned it?

What are effective strategies for monitoring student learning?

How do we respond when students are not learning?

These are only a few of the pertinent questions that should be consistently asked and answered when adults are participating in professional learning communities (PLCs). These questions can lead to rich discussion regarding ways to improve student learning, which should be the goal of every professional learning opportunity.

I still remember attending a graduate class in which, if a student's answer didn't concur with the professor's, the professor criticized the answer and humiliated the student. Isn't it funny that I remember this experience because it was personally emotional for me, and yet I don't recall any of the course content? I spent the entire semester fearing I would be called on and be unable to anticipate what the professor had in mind.

Administrators, professional developers, and college and university professors who engage adult brains with opportunities to brainstorm ideas without fear of criticism, to debate differing opinions, and to answer questions at varying levels of Bloom's taxonomy (knowledge, comprehension, application, analysis, evaluation, and synthesis) have faculty meetings and classes in which participants master amazing amounts of content and solve job-embedded problems. These are classes in which brainstorming and discussion are utilized and numerous responses are respected and valued. Refer to Figure 1.2, *Bloom's Taxonomy Revised,* at the end of this chapter for samples of question stems that can generate quality discussion.

WHY: THEORETICAL FRAMEWORK

- Teachers expressed the need for more time to talk with one another, but only 46% stated that collaboration was promoted as a part of their professional development (Gregory & Kuzmich, 2007).
- When teachers can discuss and brainstorm new ideas with other teachers in professional learning communities, they are more successful in implementing what they are learning in professional development (Nolly, 2011).
- Questions during brainstorming and discussion should be divided into two general categories: (1) those that can be answered by deductive reasoning or for which one can find the correct answer to the question by deducing it from the data provided, and (2) those that can be answered by inductive reasoning or questions to which there may be multiple solutions (Delandtsheer, 2011).
- When study groups dialogue about teaching and learning, the conversation focuses on reflection, inquiry, and exploration (Gregory, 2008).
- The purpose of discussion is to talk about something in a friendly and constructive manner while offering data, ideas, knowledge, information, and rationales for opinions and positions and attempting to convince others to accept your position (Costa, 2008).
- Following an actual experience, having people verbally retell events and ideas through discussion and dialogue assists the brain in tapping into cognitive memory (Fogarty, 2009).
- It is beneficial to adolescents and adults to have the opportunity to lead their own discussions as a group (Jensen, 2007).
- The stresses of change can be easier to manage when administrators and teachers develop teams that take on the leadership and ownership of professional learning (Gregory & Kuzmich, 2007).
- Allowing people to conduct an unguided discussion around a specific topic is an ideal way to motivate them to change and develop their knowledge, since they do not feel that they are being coerced into believing what their teacher wants them to believe (Jensen, 2007).
- When facilitating group discussions, selecting appropriate responses from the following facilitation menu may prove helpful: (1) paraphrase, (2) check for meaning, (3) give positive feedback, (4) expand or elaborate on a participant's comment, (5) increase the pace, (6) serve as the devil's advocate, (7) relieve tension, (8) consolidate by putting together ideas, (9) change the process, and (10) summarize the major views or discussions of the group (Silberman, 1999).

HOW: PROFESSIONAL LEARNING ACTIVITIES

- Have participants circulate around the room and discuss, with at least three people, their expectations for the course and what knowledge, skills, and behaviors they aspire to attain upon completion.
- Establish a participant Parking Lot as in Figure 1.1 by placing a piece of chart paper on the wall. Place four to six sticky notes on the chart paper. When participants have a question for discussion during a workshop or course, have them select a sticky note, write the question on the note, and place it back in the Parking Lot. At an appropriate time, select questions from the Parking Lot, read them aloud, and provide answers or allow participants to do so.

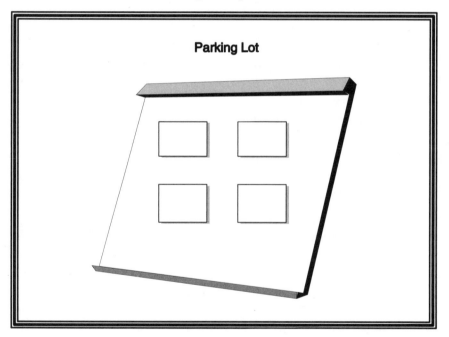

Figure 1.1

- Conduct a class session for the major purpose of exploring ideas related to a course topic or having participants offer input into the course objectives and strategies for implementation. Have participants come to class prepared to generate questions for discussion prior to teaching or participate in dialogue related to the topic.
- Give participants an open-ended question to which there may be multiple answers. Have them participate in a

brainstorming session, generating multiple ideas while adhering to the following **DOVE** guidelines: participants **D**efer judgment when others are responding, only **O**ne idea is given at a time, a **V**ariety of ideas are encouraged, and all participants are expected to direct their **E**nergy to the task.

- As content is discussed, use the *Bloom's Taxonomy Revised* question stems that follow to formulate questions at all levels. Have participants answer questions during both whole-class and small-group discussion.
- Involve participants in a Socratic Seminar during a faculty meeting or course according to the following guidelines:
  - o Determine the major concepts to be discussed from a text selection.
  - o Formulate a set of questions that encourages participants to use the higher-level thinking skills of application, analysis, evaluation, and synthesis.
  - o Have participants engaged in the discussion sit in the inner circle; note takers sit in the outer circle.
  - o To begin a discussion, start by asking a core question such as *What are the characteristics of a professional learning community?*
  - o Have participants from either the inner or outer circle conclude the discussion with a summary statement.
  - o Debrief with participants by asking for ways in which the format of the seminar could have been improved (Tanner & Cassados, 1998).
- Have participants work in cooperative groups to explain their answers to a class assignment as well as the reasoning behind the answers. When answers vary, have participants defend their answers unless convinced to change them.
- Have participants form groups based on interest in particular topics. Have each group select an article or read a book of interest to them all. Have the groups meet to discuss the content by asking questions of one another, making connections, and challenging one another's opinions.
- Have participants work in cooperative groups to brainstorm as many answers as they can come up with to a designated question. For example, during a PLC meeting, participants are asked to come up with as many ways as possible to improve the comprehension scores of fourth grade students.
- As a review activity, give participants 2 minutes to brainstorm on paper as many concepts as they can remember from a previous class session. Have them compare their brainstormed list with the

list of one of their peers. Each participant receives one point for every concept recalled that is not on his or her partner's list. The object is to accumulate as many points as possible by brainstorming a longer and more unique list.

- Have participants use the question stems of the *Bloom's Taxonomy Revised* to generate test questions that can be used for assessment purposes throughout the professional learning experience.

Bloom's Taxonomy Revised

Bloom's *Taxonomy* (1956) has stood the test of time. Recently, Anderson and Krathwohl (2001) have proposed some minor changes to include the renaming and reordering of the taxonomy. This reference reflects those recommended changes.

I. REMEMBER (KNOWLEDGE)
(shallow processing: drawing out factual answers, testing recall, and recognition)

Verbs for Objectives	Model Questions	Instructional Strategies
Choose	Who?	Highlighting
Describe	Where?	Rehearsal
Define	Which one?	Memorizing
Identify	What?	Mnemonics
Label	How?	
List	What is the best one?	
Locate	Why?	
Match	How much?	
Memorize	When?	
Name	What does it mean?	
Omit		
Recite		
Recognize		
Select		
State		

II. UNDERSTAND (COMPREHENSION)
(translating, interpreting, and extrapolating)

Verbs for Objectives	Model Questions	Instructional Strategies
Classify	State in your own words.	Key examples
Defend	What does this mean?	Emphasize connections
Demonstrate	Give an example.	Elaborate concepts
Distinguish	Condense this paragraph.	Summarize
Explain	State in one word . . .	Paraphrase
Express	What part doesn't fit?	STUDENTS explain
Extend	What exceptions are there?	STUDENTS state the rule
Give Example	What are they saying?	"Why does this example . . . ?"

(Continued)

Figure 1.2 (Continued)

Illustrate	What seems to be . . . ?	Create visual representation
Indicate	Which are facts?	(concept maps, outlines, flow
Interrelate	Is this the same as . . . ?	charts, organizers, analogies, pro/con grids) PRO/CON
Interpret	Read the graph (table).	Note: The faculty member can show them, but they have to do it.
Infer	Select the best definition.	Metaphors, rubrics, heuristics
Judge	What would happen if . . . ?	
Match	Explain what is happening.	
Paraphrase	Explain what is meant.	
Represent	What seems likely?	
Restate	This represents . . .	
Rewrite	Is it valid that . . . ?	
Select	Which statement supports . . . ?	
Show	What restrictions would you add?	
Summarize	Show in a graph or table.	
Tell		
Translate		

III. APPLY
(knowing when to apply; why to apply; and recognizing patterns of transfer to situations that are new or unfamiliar or that have a new slant for students)

Verbs for Objectives	*Model Questions*	*Instructional Strategies*
Apply	Predict what would happen if . . .	Modeling
Choose	Choose the best statements that apply.	Cognitive apprenticeships
Dramatize	Judge the effects.	"Mindful" practice—NOT just a "routine" practice
Explain	What would result?	
Generalize	Tell what would happen.	Part and whole sequencing
Judge	Tell how, when, where, why.	Authentic situations
Organize	Tell how much change there would be.	"Coached" practice
Paint	Identify the results of . . .	Case studies
Prepare		Simulations
Produce		Algorithms
Select		
Show		
Sketch		
Solve		
Use		

IV. ANALYZE (breaking down into parts, forms)

Verbs for Objectives	Model Questions	Instructional Strategies
Analyze	What is the function of . . . ?	Models of thinking
Categorize	What's fact? Opinion?	Challenging assumptions
Classify	What assumptions?	Retrospective analysis
Compare	What statement is relevant?	Reflection through journaling
Differentiate	What motive is there?	Debates
Distinguish	Related to, extraneous to, not applicable.	Discussions and other collaborating learning activities
Identify	What conclusions?	Decision-making situations
Infer	What does the author believe?	
Point Out	What does the author assume?	
Select	Make a distinction.	
Subdivide	State the point of view of . . .	
Survey	What is the premise?	
	What ideas apply?	
	What ideas justify the conclusion?	
	What's the relationship between?	
	The least essential statements are . . .	
	What's the main idea? Theme?	
	What inconsistencies, fallacies?	
	What literary form is used?	
	What persuasive technique?	
	Implicit in the statement is . . .	

V. EVALUATE (according to some set of criteria, and state why)

Verbs for Objectives	Model Questions	Instructional Strategies
Appraise	What fallacies, consistencies, or inconsistencies appear?	Challenging assumptions
Judge		Journaling
Criticize	Which is more important, moral, better, logical, valid, appropriate?	Debates
Defend	Find the errors.	Discussions and other collaborating learning activities
Compare		Decision-making situations

(Continued)

Figure 1.2 (Continued)

VI. CREATE (SYNTHESIS)
(combining elements into a pattern not clearly there before)

Verbs for Objectives	*Model Questions*	*Instructional Strategies*
Choose	How would you test . . . ?	Modeling
Combine	Propose an alternative.	Challenging assumptions
Compose	Solve the following.	Reflection through journaling
Construct	How else would you . . . ?	Debates
Create	State a rule.	Discussions and other
Design		collaborating learning activities
Develop		Design
Do		Decision-making situations
Formulate		
Hypothesize		
Invent		
Make		
Make Up		
Originate		
Organize		
Plan		
Produce		
Role Play		
Tell		

Figure 1.2   Bloom's Taxonomy Revised

Source: Anderson & Krathwohl, 2001. Compiled by the IUPUI Center for Teaching and Learning. Revised December 2002. Used with permission.

REFLECTION AND APPLICATION

> How will I incorporate *brainstorming and discussion*
> into professional learning to engage participants' brains?

Which brainstorming and discussion activities am I already incorporating into my professional learning?

What additional brainstorming and discussion activities will I incorporate?

<h1>Strategy 2</h1>

<h1>Drawing and Artwork</h1>

WHAT: DEFINING THE STRATEGY

When the famous artist Pablo Picasso turned in his textbooks upon flunking out of school, the pages were covered in doodles. How many times have you witnessed adults who are doodling on a piece of scratch paper or along the margins of their notes while sitting in a workshop, especially if they were bored? These participants may have what Howard Gardner (1983) calls spatial intelligence.

Consider the alternative. Have you ever asked an adult to draw something, especially something creative, just to be met with the comment, *I can't draw!* Isn't it sad that the creativity many of us believed we possessed as children was not nurtured after kindergarten, so that many adults truly think that they are incapable of producing anything artistic? Yet more than 75 years ago, John Dewey (1934) told us that the thinking in which we engage while producing art precedes improved thinking across the curriculum.

In my workshops, adults draw a human body to remind them that procedural memory involves the use of the body, a smiley face to recall that positive thinking strengthens memory and immunity, and a face with a frown to symbolize the threats that extreme stress, anger, and fear can have on both the brain and body. Why not involve your adult brains in a plethora of artistic activities to demonstrate what they are learning? Allow them to draw, color, and create their way toward new knowledge and skills.

WHY: THEORETICAL FRAMEWORK

- Learners need to be exposed to a variety of ways to express themselves artistically (Jensen, 2008).
- The shared emotion between the painter and those who see the work of art not only assists in maintaining important cognitive systems but also increases the awareness and development of social skills (Sylwester, 2010).
- When people draw or add doodles to their notes, they create visuals that help them understand, process or encode information, and recall new information as well (Allen, 2008a).
- Artwork and drawing are good ways to explore emotions and even better ways to manage states and channel energy and concentration (Jensen, 2008).
- Human beings are the only creatures capable of combining symbols (such as dots and squiggles) to derive meaning and, therefore, to create culture (Medina, 2008).
- Drawing pictures and pictographs is one activity that aids in the nonlinguistic (or mental) processing of information (Marzano, 2007).
- The ability to draw is actually a person's ability to see edges, spaces, lights and shadows, relationships, and the whole (Edwards, 1999).
- The use of patterns found in art, music, dance, and drama can assist the brain in its search for meaning (Fogarty, 2001).
- Various areas of the brain, including the thalamus and the amygdala, are activated when people are involved in art activities (Jensen, 2001).
- Thinking in art precedes improvements in thinking in other curricular areas (Dewey, 1934).

HOW: PROFESSIONAL LEARNING ACTIVITIES

- Many participants will doodle while attending your workshop. Let them! It is one way that many adults process information. Show some of your participants' drawings to the class as examples of how adults master content through the strategy of drawing and artwork.
- As you teach, incorporate simple drawings into your presentation. Draw a concept on the board or document camera and have your participants copy the drawing in their notes to help them recall the concept. For example, when teaching the need for movement while learning, I have participants draw a body to indicate that anything learned while the body is moving is remembered longer.
- As a review activity, have participants work in groups of four to six to create a wall mural or graffiti to symbolize their understanding of content previously learned.

- Have participants illustrate the meaning of a key vocabulary word previously taught. For example, when I teach the vocabulary word *knout* (which is a *whip*), I have participants draw a *knout* to help them remember the definition.

- Stop, when appropriate, and have participants illustrate a major concept previously taught. For example, to depict their comprehension of the term *block schedule*, have administrators work in small groups to actually design one. After all, *one learns to do by doing!*

- During a strategic or school-improvement planning session, have participants work in cooperative groups of four to six to draw a scene depicting what their school or school system should look like when its mission has been achieved. A representative from each group should explain the group's drawing to the entire staff.

- Have participants draw a stick figure and attach notes to it regarding eight categories of a person, group of people being studied, or a school or school system. To the brain, they attach ideas; to the eyes, vision; to the mouth, words; to the hands, actions; to the heart, feelings; to the feet, movement; to the Achilles' tendon, weaknesses; and to the arm muscle, strengths (Sousa, 2001).

- During a leadership professional learning experience, have participants either draw or cut pictures from magazines that depict their leadership style. Have them paste the selected pictures onto a collage that is displayed during the class. Place participants in small groups and have them individually explain how their collage exemplifies their leadership style. You can adapt the same activity to have teachers depict their personality styles.

- During a workshop where the participants are mentors or peer or instructional coaches, have them work in groups of four to six to either draw or cut pictures from magazines that depict the characteristics the group thinks are essential in an effective mentor or coach. Have them paste the selected pictures onto a collage that is displayed during the class. Have a representative from each group explain how their collage exemplifies the ideal coach or mentor.

- As you lecture on concepts that can be quite complicated, draw a graphic organizer or mind map that shows how the ideas are connected. Have participants draw the graphic organizer along with you in their notes for ready reference when the concepts need to be reviewed. Consult *Strategy 5: Graphic Organizers, Semantic Maps, and Word Webs* for sample mind or concept maps.

REFLECTION AND APPLICATION

> How will I incorporate *drawing and artwork*
> into professional learning to engage participants' brains?

Which drawing and artwork activities am I already incorporating into my professional learning?

What additional drawing and artwork activities will I incorporate?

Strategy 3

Field Trips

WHAT: DEFINING THE STRATEGY

R ecently, I was the keynote speaker at New Teacher Orientation in Omaha, Nebraska. I had the privilege of engaging 200 beginning teachers in activities that I believed would enable them to have a successful first year. I modeled for them what they should be doing with their students, including greeting them at the door, playing calming music when they arrived, and having them talking and moving to learn the content. You see, even keynotes need to be highly engaging! I showed them how to have their students make appointments to discuss important concepts, how to incorporate movement into their own lessons, and how to manage an active classroom without ever raising their voices.

What was most impressive to me, however, was the fact that once the opening program had ended, these 200 new teachers were put on school buses and taken on a tour of the neighborhoods from which their students would come. This field trip would enable teachers to see firsthand where their students and parents live, work, and play. I cannot think of a more valuable experience!

Research suggests that professional developers, administrators, or college professors who plan and execute field trips enable their students to apply theory and knowledge (Jensen & Dabney, 2000). These field trips, however, must be directly related to a standard or content objective and should be taken prior to the unit of instruction. In this way, the brain can make connections between what was experienced on the field trips and the subsequent learning.

Virtual field trips, a viable option today, enable participants to journey to distant locations and never leave the comfort of the classroom. Receiving pertinent information from the state department of education at a faculty meeting, experiencing a math or science lesson from a master teacher in another location, or communicating with teachers from across the country while sitting in one's own school is not only possible but very feasible (see *Strategy 16: Technology*).

If all else fails and class participants cannot go to the source of study, then the source of study may be invited to come to class. When guests are invited to come and speak on pertinent topics, they provide links between the content being learned and its application in the real world. For example, asking principals to form a panel and share their daily experiences in a leadership academy class is much more memorable and brain compatible than simply reading about what the job of an administrator must be like.

WHY: THEORETICAL FRAMEWORK

- One way that teachers can integrate planned movement while learning content is to take a field trip (Sprenger, 2007).
- The information that teachers glean from home visits to their students' families and the conversations that they engage in contribute to the relationships between families and teachers to enhance student learning (Ginsberg, 2011).
- A field trip is an example of an actual experience that taps into a student's spatial memory, the time or place that something actually occurred (Fogarty, 2009).
- As teachers make home visits in communities that are constantly changing, educators become more familiar with the strengths of students' families and can see how the personal stories of those families can make curriculum more relevant to students (Ginsberg, 2011).
- Electronic field trips can be more beneficial than real field trips because they expand the learning outside the walls of the classroom, and an event can be experienced more than once (Gregory & Herndon, 2010).
- Field trips, even virtual ones, create spatial memories that end up being embedded in the brain and need no rehearsal (Fogarty, 2001).
- Much of the information stored in the brain comes from concrete experience, not necessarily from association (Westwater & Wolfe, 2000).
- Critical thinking skills can be improved by getting participants out of the classroom and into the real world (Jensen & Dabney, 2000).
- Aristotle and Socrates, two of the world's greatest teachers, used field trips thousands of years ago as tools of instruction (Krepel & Duvall, 1981).

HOW: PROFESSIONAL LEARNING ACTIVITIES

- Field trips do not have to cost money. When the weather conditions are conducive, convene class in a different location rather than the four walls of the classroom to take advantage of novel and different surroundings, such as meeting outside under a tree or going to a nearby park.

- Have teachers new to the school board a bus, as they did in Omaha, and take a field trip to the communities from which their students will come. This trip can provide insights regarding where students live, what is available in their communities, and where their parents might work.

- Select a site relevant to course content and have participants visit it prior to a unit of study so that they can have real-life experiences to assist them in making the subsequent content meaningful.

- Have teachers who want or need to learn new strategies for classroom management or instructional delivery visit the classrooms of teachers with exemplary skills in those areas. A mentor, peer coach, or administrator may want to accompany the visiting teacher during the observation so that a conversation can ensue. Prior to the conference, the visiting teacher can talk with the mentor regarding what specific things to look for and, following the observation, debrief about what was observed.

- Have teachers in a professional learning experience take a field trip to a classroom or a school where exemplary instruction is modeled daily. For example, I live in Atlanta, Georgia, where the Ron Clark Academy is located. This school has become famous for its ability to make exemplary academic gains with its students. A movie, *The Ron Clark Story*, has even been made about its founder. Teachers come from all over the country to visit the Ron Clark Academy and see firsthand how it's done.

- Have social studies teachers take a field trip to a local museum or historical site to acquire information that will strengthen their content knowledge about a particular culture or period of history. For example, participants in a course on Egyptian civilization can visit the Carlos Museum on the campus of Emory University in Atlanta, Georgia.

- Have science teachers journey to a region under study to acquire additional content knowledge or to observe first-hand the characteristics of landforms such as swamps, marshlands, or mountains.
- Have participants view distance-learning telecasts concerning a particular course objective, such as watching a science experiment being performed in a distant location.
- Connect to the Internet and type the words *field trip* into a search engine. You will discover many sites that allow you to plan a virtual field trip for your adult learners.

REFLECTION AND APPLICATION

> How will I incorporate *field trips* into
> professional learning to engage participants' brains?

Which field trips am I already incorporating into my professional learning?

What additional field trips will I incorporate?

<h1>Strategy 4</h1>

<h1>Games</h1>

WHAT: DEFINING THE STRATEGY

One of the highlights of my Worksheets Don't Grow Dendrites workshop is a spirited ball game during which one participant from each group, or family, tosses a ball to a participant in another family who is standing at a distance, and then sits down. What makes the game so much fun is that you cannot throw the ball to anyone standing near you, and if the ball hits the floor at any time during the game, everyone who sat down stands back up and the game starts all over again. Family members are allowed to help one another, and the energy level in the workshop increases by at least 50%. You should see people diving for the ball so that they do not disappoint their family and the game can continue. During a conference presentation in Philadelphia, one science coordinator was determined that she would not let the ball hit the floor when it came to her so she dove for the ball. However, in doing so, her table and water pitcher ended up on the floor. The good news is that no one got wet or hurt. The better news is that she caught the ball and the game continued. No one will ever forget that spirited ball game!

In my classes, adults have fun! In fact, as I stand and greet them at the door, so many participants who have attended my classes before come in the door sharing with me how excited they are to be back. More importantly, however, adults in my workshops learn a great deal and appear to retain what they have learned for long periods of time.

Don't forget the time-tested saying, *You don't stop playing games because you grow old. You grow old because you stop playing games.* The moment adults decide that they should stop having fun is the day they begin to grow old. No one grows older in my professional development experiences!

WHY: THEORETICAL FRAMEWORK

- Regardless of the age of the student, physically engaging games can greatly improve the brain's ability to learn (Allen, 2008a).
- Putting the content into review games makes the review fun (Jensen & Nickelsen, 2008).
- Many of the games we learned as kids can be adapted by teachers and used in the classroom to bring content to life while having people physically moving (Baumgarten, 2006).
- Games must focus on academic content if they are going to represent a way to review that content (Marzano, 2007).
- Since games, puzzles, and other fun activities can make the content more creative, they should be used when students have to memorize, practice, or rehearse crucial information (Caine, Caine, McClintic, & Klimek, 2009).
- Games stimulate attention since they involve missing information (Marzano, 2007).
- Play involves the built-in processes of challenge, novelty, feedback, coherence, and time, which all enable the brain to mature faster (Jensen, 2001).
- A game is more effective when those who are planning to play it actually construct it (Wolfe, 2001).
- Physical games engage people of any age socially, mentally, and emotionally (Summerford, 2000).
- Play establishes specific myelinated pathways between the frontal lobe and the limbic system, representing the full integration of mind and body (Hannaford, 2005).
- Playing games is one of the 10 things that keep people living beyond the age of 80 (Mahoney, 2005).

HOW: PROFESSIONAL LEARNING ACTIVITIES

- Play the game Facts in Four as a get-acquainted activity. Have participants write down four facts related to them personally. Three of the facts should be true and one false. Participants should not use true facts that other participants already know (e.g., *I teach chemistry at _____ school).* The purpose of the game is to keep peers from guessing which is the false fact. To fool them, each participant should select unique true facts and create believable false ones. Participants take turns reading their four facts aloud and having class members guess the false one. If the group is too large, this game can be played in small groups rather than with the entire class.

When I play Facts and Four, I model what participants are supposed to do by telling my four facts. See if you can guess which one is the false fact:

1. I am an avid sports fan.
2. I was born in the elevator of a local hospital.
3. I have presented on four of the seven continents.
4. I own 65 episodes of the *Columbo* television series.

If you ever meet me, I will be happy to tell you which one is the false fact.

- Place participants in cooperative groups. Give each group a generic game board with a minimum of 25 spaces, including *move forward* and *go back* spaces. Provide game cards containing questions related to course content. Have group members take turns rolling a number generator (a die), selecting a game card, and answering the designated question on the card (such as *Name an instructional strategy that engages students* or *State a question at the "application" level of Bloom's taxonomy*). If the question is answered correctly, the participant moves the marker forward the rolled number of spaces. If the answer is incorrect, the participant is not allowed to move. The first player in each group to reach the end of the game is the winner.
- Construct a facsimile of the television game show *Jeopardy!* by selecting important facts related to the objectives of the workshop or course. Answers are placed on a board or on index cards in 100-, 200-, 300-, 400-, and 500-point categories. The easiest answers are worth 100 points; the most difficult are worth 500 points. Three answers are placed under each category for a total of 15 questions. Participants form three teams, select a spokesperson, and take turns supplying the question to the answer selected. The game proceeds according to the rules of the television game show *Jeopardy!* Be sure to include two *Daily Doubles* to make the game more interesting. Any team that has points at the end of the round can wager any or all of it on a bonus question (the most difficult

question to be asked). This game can also be played via the computer.

- Have participants play Charades by having their peers guess the key concept or term they are pantomiming. The first person to guess correctly is selected to act out the next concept.

- Provide participants with a Bingo card containing 16 blank spaces. Select 25 to 30 pertinent vocabulary concepts from the course and have participants randomly write any 16 of the words on their cards. Write a definition for each word on an index card and place the cards in a bag. Have participants take turns drawing a definition of one concept from the bag and reading the definition aloud. Have participants cover the corresponding word as its definition is read. The first person to cover four words in a row either vertically, horizontally, or diagonally shouts out *Bingo!* and wins the game.

- Conduct a simple Ball Toss game by having participants stand and form a circle. Stand in the center of the circle. Ask a question related to what you have taught to the entire class. Give participants at least 5 seconds to think of an answer. Then randomly throw the ball to a person in the circle who must give the answer. That person then throws the ball to another person who will answer the next question. If the group is too large, have participants play who fit a certain category, such as all participants who are born in the month of June, while the rest of the class watches and cheers.

- Have participants work in cooperative groups to develop an original game or revise an existing one to demonstrate their understanding of course content. Each group determines the name of the game, the game's rules and regulations, and how the winner is determined. The entire class plays the game as content is reviewed and retained.

- Since your class may already be put into cooperative groups, or families, take advantage of that structure. When you need someone to participate in an activity in front of the entire class, give points to the family if a group member volunteers. Any family that reaches a predetermined number of points can participate in a celebration at the end of class. Celebrations are usually designated movements designed to review content or signal success. You would be surprised how even adult brains volunteer when they anticipate receiving points for their effort!

REFLECTION AND APPLICATION

How will I incorporate *games* into
professional learning to engage participants' brains?

Which games am I already incorporating into my professional learning?

What additional games will I incorporate?

Strategy 5

Graphic Organizers, Semantic Maps, and Word Webs

WHAT: DEFINING THE STRATEGY

One of the major parts of the *Sit and Get Won't Grow Dendrites* workshop is a section that enables teachers of the adult brain to understand the five things that every participant should be doing if the presenter wants them to grow brain cells, or dendrites. In other words, these five actions help to ensure that the content from the professional learning will stand a better chance of being remembered. Instead of presenting this information in a linear fashion, such as an outline, I use the graphic organizer or mind map, shown in Figure 5.1, which clarifies the major points and delineates the details under each point. To add clarification, I put the main ideas in boxes and write them with blue ink, while the details under each main idea are not put in boxes and are written in black ink. Color-coding certain topics can be very helpful to memory. I have participants draw the mind map along with me as I explain each fact. Each of the facts presented also has an activity inherent in it so that the entire section of the presentation is not simply a lecture but has participants actively engaged.

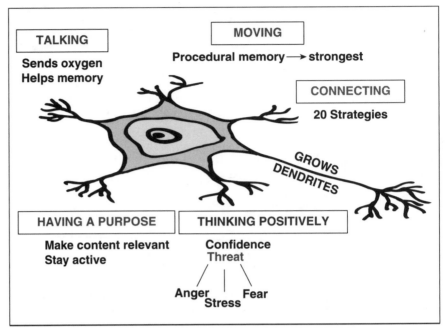

Figure 5.1

Developed by Tony Buzan (1993), chairman of the Brain Foundation, mind maps or graphic organizers, by their very nature, are brain compatible since they appeal to both left and right hemispheres. They are pictorial representations of linear ideas and show the connectedness of content. Any time I have a concept to teach that can be complicated or relatively difficult to understand, a graphic organizer is in order.

WHY: THEORETICAL FRAMEWORK

- Thinking maps have the following five critical attributes: (1) a consistent form that reflects the skill being addressed; (2) a flexible way the map can be configured; (3) a developmental form that can increase in complexity; (4) an integration of content knowledge with thinking processes; and (5) a reflection of the learner's thinking processes (Hyerle & Alper, 2011).
- Concept mapping gives the brain an opportunity to integrate theory with professional practice, promotes organizational skills and problem solving, and is, therefore, a good metacognitive strategy (Materna, 2007).
- "Graphic organizers make thinking and learning visible" (Fogarty, 2009, p. 112).
- Creating mind maps, or open-ended depictions of thought, reinforces understanding of relationships and associations between ideas and provides an effective vehicle for evaluating learning (Jensen, 2008).
- When people create their own graphic organizers, those organizers become more memorable because people conceptualize and design them and are intimately connected to them (Allen, 2008a).

- Graphic organizers, pictures, graphs, and charts are effective tools by which people can organize patterns, since images are more easily remembered by the brain than are words (Feinstein, 2009).
- Adult learners are naturally self-directed, and graphic organizers encourage this autonomy (Materna, 2007).
- Graphic organizers cannot only be used as prereading and prewriting tools since they facilitate discussion and note taking, they can also be used following the reading of narrative and expository texts as summary or synthesis tools (Perez, 2008).
- Graphic organizers facilitate the acquisition of new knowledge and can help the learner discern discrepancies between new knowledge and that previously learned (Materna, 2007).
- A graphic organizer called a Fishbone diagram can enable a group to identify solutions or effects and systematically examine possible causes (Delehant, 2007).

HOW: PROFESSIONAL LEARNING ACTIVITIES

- Have participants use the Venn diagram shown in Figure 5.2 anytime two or more parallel concepts are being compared or contrasted. For example, the following graphic organizer is the ideal tool for comparing and contrasting traditional assessment and authentic or performance assessment. Ways in which the two concepts are alike are included in the inner circle. Differences are reflected in the two outer circles.

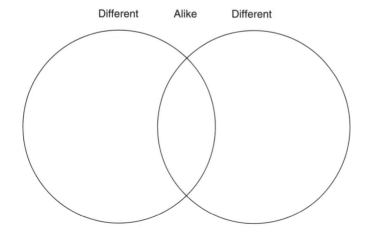

Compare/Contrast

Different   Alike   Different

Figure 5.2

- A web organizer has a multitude of uses. Have participants utilize the web shown in Figure 5.3 when brainstorming ideas, recalling facts about a particular topic previously discussed, delineating the main idea and details of a concept, or showing a vocabulary word and its synonyms. For example, when examining student data during a professional learning community meeting, instructional priorities could be identified and written on the web for all to consider.

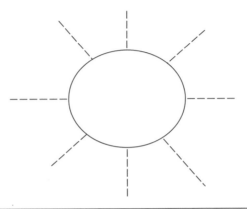

Figure 5.3

- Have participants utilize a sequence chart like the one in Figure 5.4 whenever events need to be prioritized or placed in sequential order or on a timeline. For example, a school faculty could take the ideas generated during a school-improvement planning session and place them on an implementation timeline through the use of this chart.

Sequence

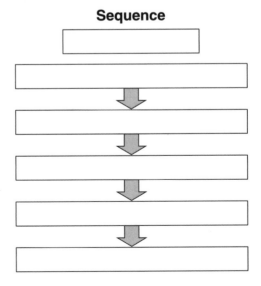

Figure 5.4

- When teaching a concept that may be difficult to comprehend, create mind maps like the one in Figure 5.5 to assist participants in seeing the connections between the ideas presented. Participants can then create their own mind or semantic maps to demonstrate their understanding of a presented concept. The more colorful, visual, and symbolic the mind map, the more brain compatible it is.

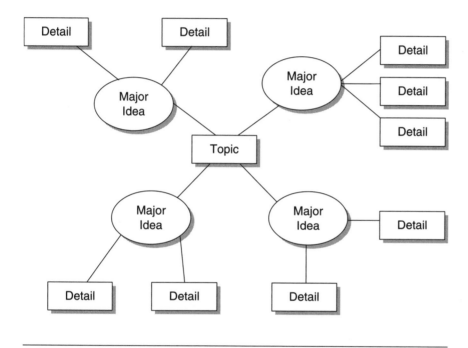

Figure 5.5

- Have participants prioritize ideas through the use of the ranking ladder organizer (see Figure 5.6). For example, following a departmental meeting at which ideas for increasing student achievement are brainstormed, each teacher could place the top four ideas on the ladder in order of priority. Group consensus can then be reached regarding the top idea(s) to be implemented.
- When participants are preparing to debate a controversial issue, the agree-disagree chart (see Figure 5.7) is helpful. Have participants brainstorm reasons they agree or disagree with the issue. Those reasons are recorded on the organizer and then discussed.

Ranking Ladder

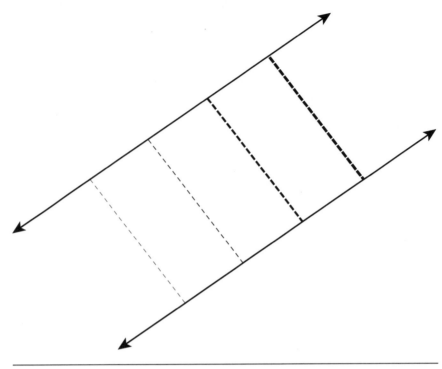

Figure 5.6

Agree-Disagree Chart

Issue	Agree	Disagree

Figure 5.7

- Have participants use the fishbone organizer (see Figure 5.8) to break down a concept into its critical attributes, demonstrate past to present events, or even show cause and effect. For example, have participants list the critical attributes of a brain-compatible learning environment. The first tier of the fishbone could list attributes of the physical environment (e.g., color, music, lighting). The second tier could list teacher attributes (e.g., positive interactions, high expectations, knowledgeable).

Fishbone

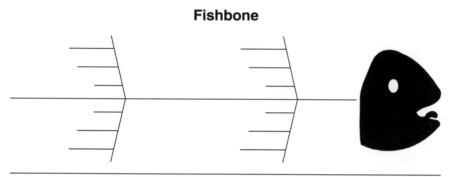

Figure 5.8

- Have participants use a pie chart like the one in Figure 5.9 when attempting to discern what percentage of the faculty or community agrees with a particular idea expressed by someone in the group or a recommendation for implementation, such as *Should our students wear school uniforms?*

Pie Chart

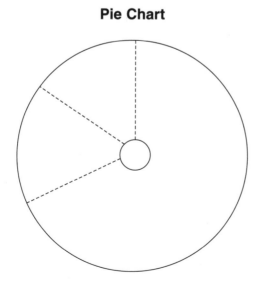

Figure 5.9

- When reteaching a concept to a partner or group or comprehending content, have participants develop their own graphic organizers to facilitate comprehension. For example, in a session in which I had to teach one of Learning Forward's professional learning standards to a partner, I designed a graphic organizer to show the cycle a professional learning community experiences. This cycle organizer is shown in Figure 5.10.

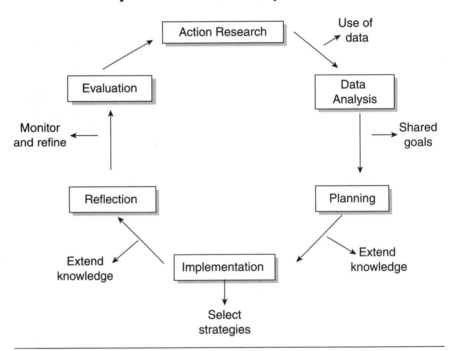

Cycle of Continuous Improvement

Figure 5.10

REFLECTION AND APPLICATION

How will I incorporate *graphic organizers, semantic maps, and word webs* into professional learning to engage participants' brains?

Which graphic organizers, semantic maps, and word webs am I already incorporating into my professional learning?

What additional activities will I incorporate?

Strategy 6

Humor and Celebration

WHAT: DEFINING THE STRATEGY

I remember a few years ago when I was presenting to a group of teachers in Sevierville, Tennessee. Something happened that I will never forget! My audience was having a great time while actively engaged in the workshop when a man came to the door and asked to speak to a teacher in the audience. She was summoned and went to see what the man wanted. A few minutes later, the woman returned, visibly upset, gathered her belongings and left the class. I later inquired and found out that the teacher had just received word that her favorite nephew had been killed in Afghanistan. How devastated she was, and so were we!

It would not have mattered how well I taught for the remainder of the day, that teacher's brain would not have heard a word I said. You see, her brain suddenly shifted into survival mode and could care less about anything academic at that point. Maslow was absolutely correct! *The brain learns best when not in high stress!* Leaders who lead by threatening their staffs have employees whose brains stay in survival mode and who can eventually lose their creativity and enthusiasm for the profession.

Teaching is hard work, and when your audience gathers, especially after a full day of instruction, begin your professional learning experience with a cartoon or joke. Humor puts the brain in a positive state for learning, encourages creativity, and can make your professional learning experience memorable for the right reason.

In addition, adults do not typically celebrate success unless they are in sports. Have you ever seen football players get excited when a teammate scores a touchdown or soccer players run out on the field and jump on top of the person who scored the winning goal? In fact, sometimes athletes can be charged with excessive celebration! As faculties accomplish student outcomes and objectives and move toward increases in student achievement, celebrations should be the order of the day!

WHY: THEORETICAL FRAMEWORK

- When it comes to training, audiences value the ability of a presenter to moderate behavior with humor and skill (Jensen & Nickelsen, 2008).
- Members of an organization are more likely to embrace the purpose and work toward mutual priorities when celebrations continue to remind people of the purpose and priorities (Dufour et al., 2011).
- During a workshop, particularly one facilitated at the end of a long day, humor has the potential to relieve tension and reduce stress (Nash, 2010).
- Celebrations allow for an organization to express appreciation (which lets others know that they received something of value) and admiration (which enables staff members to be inspired by observing the work and commitment of others; Dufour et al., 2010).
- Workshop facilitators may make fun of themselves but never of anyone else. Being sarcastic to participants encourages them to be sarcastic to you (Nash, 2010).
- Even small improvements in behavior along the way should be rewarded. It is not necessary to wait until people achieve extraordinary results (Patterson et al., 2008).
- Laughter can be considered a form of internal jogging since it gets the blood circulating, the lungs moving, the blood pressure and stress-hormone levels lowering, and results in lessening the chances of having a second heart attack for those who have had one previously (Kluger, 2005).
- An emerging body of research is showing that the risk of social and psychological factors such as stress, anxiety, depression, and hostility has about as great an impact on the medical markers for cardiovascular disease as do smoking, obesity, and hypertension (Underwood, 2005).
- Laughter, fake or real, is one of the 10 things that keep people living beyond the age of 80 (Mahoney, 2005).
- Humor is not inherited but acquired and influenced by people's values, temperament, background, and the situation in which they find themselves, as well as the people surrounding them (Burgess, 2000).
- Laughter can make the school day shorter, lighten the load, help people to cope with crisis, break up monotony, and lengthen one's life (Burgess, 2000).
- Humor can have a very positive effect on a meeting's outcome right from the start, since it loosens up the participants and sends them thinking along different lines (Silberman, 1999).

HOW: PROFESSIONAL LEARNING ACTIVITIES

- Help to ensure participant success by stating the purpose of the learning experience at the beginning, including what participants should know and be able to do upon completion of the learning objectives.
- Post humorous or meaningful sayings or cartoons on the wall that exemplify messages for participant success. Some sample sayings could include the following:
    - *The brain learns best when it is not in high stress!*
    - *If your students like you, there is nothing they will not do for you. If your students don't like you, there is nothing they will not do to you!*
    - *Without hope for tomorrow, there is no strength for today!*
- Adults will not always volunteer to take the lead role in a cooperative group or supply an answer for the class. When it is time to select a spokesperson for a group, have participants point into the air and then, on the count of three, have them point to the person in the group that they want to be the spokesperson. The participant in each group with the most fingers pointing at her or him becomes the spokesperson and supplies the answer. Take it from me, participants always laugh heartily at this point!
- When groups need to report to the class following a cooperative learning activity, select a spokesperson according to the following additional categories:
    - Participants dressed in blue (or any other color)
    - Participants wearing contact lenses or glasses
    - Participants wearing the most jewelry
    - Participants with the shortest/longest hair
    - Participants who have the greatest number of siblings, children, or pets
    - Participants who have been in education the longest/shortest length of time
    - Participants who drove the farthest/least far to get to the training location

Here is a funny story. I had asked the person in each group who had the longest hair to report to the class regarding the group's findings. One teacher raised her hand and in all sincerity asked me this question, *Does the hair have to be yours?* I replied, *It is yours if you have a receipt for it.* The entire class laughed.

Participants may create additional humorous categories for selecting peers to fulfill other cooperative group roles (i.e. facilitator, recorder/scribe, resource manager, timekeeper).

- Integrate humor into your professional learning with jokes that are appropriate for the content you are teaching. I typically tell at least four jokes, one at the beginning of class, one following each break, and one after lunch. If I have the same group of adults for more than one day, I provide the jokes for the first day and then ask for volunteers to be the class clowns for the remaining days. You would be surprised at the quality of the jokes that adults prepare and deliver. Some missed their calling. They should have been stand-up comedians!

- Riddles work very well to add humor to your professional learning experience. In fact, adults have to think at very high levels to solve some riddles. Here are some of the ones I use related to content:

  o What did the number zero say to the number eight? *Nice belt.*
  o How do you tell the sex of a chromosome? *Just pull down their jeans (genes).*
  o Why do you never want to date a tennis player? *To them, love means nothing.*
  o Which flower does not grow in the ground? *The* Mayflower.
  o What did the green grape say to the purple grape? *Breathe! Breathe!*

- If you are not comfortable with your ability to deliver a joke, then use cartoons that are appropriate to your content. A great source for cartoons related to education would be the series of books by Aaron Bacall published by Corwin. His books are as follows:

  o *The Lighter Side of Classroom Management*
  o *The Lighter Side of Educational Leadership*
  o *The Lighter Side of Staff Development*
  o *The Lighter Side of Teaching*
  o *The Lighter Side of Technology*

"Now we will reinforce the key points in a compelling way, using humor. Please put on the clown makeup and nose provided in each training kit."

- Show appreciation for correct participant responses in humorous ways, such as high-fiving them, providing applause with a plastic hand clapper, or shining the light on them with a magic wand that makes noise. The wand can be purchased at the web site www.tool-trainers.com.

- Have participants who are working in cooperative groups create an original cheer to be used when the group experiences success during the workshop. The cheer should take only 1 or 2 seconds. Groups take turns performing their cheers for the class. Then, when the entire class has success, all the groups perform their cheers simultaneously.

- After participants successfully complete a learning segment or at the end of a workshop, play music that symbolizes a celebration of the content learned, such as Handel's *Hallelujah Chorus*, Kool and the Gang's "Celebration," or the theme from the movie *Rocky*. Coincidentally, as I am writing this chapter, they are playing the theme from the movie *Rocky* during the fifth game of the National League Championship series between the Saint Louis Cardinals and the Philadelphia Phillies to encourage confidence in the players and the crowd.

- Following documented increases in student achievement, encourage teachers to celebrate their successes! Celebrations might include, but are not limited to, special recognitions in faculty meetings, dining together with a pot luck lunch or dinner, covering a teacher's class so that he or she can have some quiet, relaxing time, or giving gift certificates donated by school community partners or adopters.

REFLECTION AND APPLICATION

How will I incorporate *humor and celebration* into professional learning to engage participants' brains?

Which humorous and celebratory activities am I already incorporating into my professional learning?

What additional activities will I incorporate?

Strategy 7

Manipulatives and Models

WHAT: DEFINING THE STRATEGY

Iwas recently presenting in Norman, Oklahoma, at Moore Norman Technology Center to a group of college professors when, prior to the start of my workshop, a team-building activity was conducted. The professors were grouped in the professional learning teams that they had worked in all year. Each team was given a bag containing the following identical materials: 1 large marshmallow, 20 pieces of uncooked spaghetti, 1 yard of masking tape, and 1 yard of string. The goal for each team was to work together to construct the tallest freestanding structure possible using only the items in the bag. The challenge was that the marshmallow had to reside on the top of the structure. Each group was given 18 minutes to complete the task. I provided the music so that while the groups worked, they listened to the high-energy tunes from the greatest hits of Michael MacDonald.

After 18 minutes, teams shared their final products. Only one group was able to construct a structure that would withstand the weight of the large marshmallow on top. What a wonderful opportunity to observe the team-building tactics of each group! Following the activity, a video was shown regarding research on which groups actually perform better on this task in general. Guess which ones do the best work. Not professionals! Not people with earned doctorates! You guessed it—kindergartners. Maybe you didn't guess it. I know I didn't! But when you really think about it—everything you needed to know you actually learned in kindergarten! After all, the very best teaching methodologies combine both mind and body (Wilson, 1999). Anything less may be appropriate for short-term memory but not necessarily for long-term retention.

WHY: THEORETICAL FRAMEWORK

- The concrete visuals that can be touched and manipulated are the ones that are best remembered (Jensen, 2008).
- Making physical models is one activity that aids in the nonlinguistic (or mental) processing of information (Marzano, 2007).
- Many people learn best when activities are hands on and they are able to manipulate physical objects and concepts (Jensen, 2008).
- Information is better remembered and neural connections more easily formed when learning is active and hands on than when information is learned abstractly or when students are watching the teacher do all the work (Gregory & Parry, 2006).
- People increase their abilities to verbalize their thinking, discuss ideas, take ownership, and find answers to problems on their own when they use manipulatives over time (Sebesta & Martin, 2004).
- The use of the hands and activity in the brain is such a complicated connection that no one theory explains it (Jensen, 2001).
- For some people, thinking and learning are enhanced through the power of touch (Jonson, 2002).
- Hands-on learning is implicit, which makes it long term, cross-cultural, independent of age, simple to acquire, and independent of measures of intelligence (Jensen, 2001).
- There could be a link between the absence of touch and lowered levels of the neurotransmitter acetylcholine exhibited by Alzheimer's patients (Hannaford, 2005).
- Professions such as sculpting, mechanics, and surgery enable adults to use their hands either to create or change things in the real world (Armstrong, 1994).

HOW: PROFESSIONAL LEARNING ACTIVITIES

- Interact tactilely with participants through handshakes, high fives, and pats on the back. A good time to implement this will be when you are greeting participants at the door prior to the beginning of the workshop. Communicating with participants through the power of touch can assist in creating the positive climate so essential for optimal learning.

- Stop periodically during the workshop and have participants affirm their partners or others in their groups, or families, by shaking hands, giving them a high five, or patting one another on the back.
- Have participants demonstrate tactically their agreement or disagreement with an answer or their levels of understanding for an answer by doing one of the following:
  - Thumbs up—agree
  - Thumbs down—disagree
  - Five fingers—completely understand
  - One finger—don't understand
  - Pat head—understand
  - Scratch head—don't understand

Source: Tate, 2010.

- Give participants two 3 × 5 index cards of different colors and a piece of tape. Have them tape the cards together, back to back. Have participants write the word *YES* on one color card and the word *NO* on the other. Whenever there is a need for a response in the workshop or meeting, have participants hold up either the *YES* or *NO* card to show agreement or disagreement.
- Provide participants with dry-erase boards on which they can respond in writing to designated questions during a workshop or meeting. If the group is large, have participants work in groups with one participant serving as the scribe and writing the group's answer on the dry-erase board.
- During a professional learning community meeting, when teachers are asked to indicate a level of support for a recommended proposal, use the following *Fist to Five Strategy:*

  5 Fingers: *I love this proposal and will champion it.*

  4 Fingers: *I strongly agree with the proposal.*

  3 Fingers: *The proposal is okay with me. I am willing to go along.*

  2 Fingers: *I have reservations and am not yet ready to support this proposal.*

  1 Finger: *I am opposed to this proposal.*

  Fist: *If I had the authority, I would veto this proposal, regardless of the will of the group.*

Source: Dufour et al., 2010, p. 229.

- Have participants work individually or in cooperative groups to demonstrate their understanding of a concept by placing manipulatives in proper categories. For example, following a discussion of the four personality characteristics in the course *True Colors*, give participants an envelope containing four cards with the color headings Gold, Blue, Green, and Orange, as well as 30 cards representing various personality or temperament types. Have participants sort each personality characteristic under the proper heading.

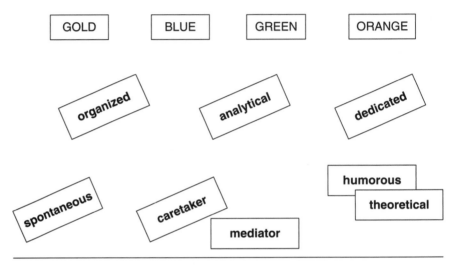

Figure 7.1

- Have participants construct a model to demonstrate their understanding of a concept previously taught in class. For example, when teaching participants during a mathematics content course, have them stretch rubber bands over peg boards to create a variety of geometric patterns.
- Have participants use their hands to demonstrate major concepts that are being taught in a workshop or course. For example, when teaching the three parts of a neuron, or memory cell, have them wiggle their fingers to simulate a dendrite, tap the palm of their hand to indicate the cell body, and tap the arm to simulate the axon.
- During a course in which participants are learning a new technological application, have each participant demonstrate knowledge by performing the application on his or her assigned computer. It will not be sufficient for them to watch as you demonstrate the application on a projected screen.

Following the course, have each participant return to the workplace and consistently apply the content learned in an assigned project or on-the-job application. Remember, *One learns to do by doing!*

- Divide participants in grade-level or departmental groups. When studying the Common Core State Standards, have groups select a targeted standard taught at their grade level and trace the standard through the grades below and above the designated grade. Have them note how the standard changes as students progress through the grade levels. Then have teachers write the noted changes on strips of paper and tape those strips to the wall in grade-level progression so that teachers can immediately see how their instruction fits in the overall scheme of mastery.

REFLECTION AND APPLICATION

How will I incorporate *manipulatives and models* into professional learning to engage participants' brains?

Which manipulatives and models am I already incorporating into my professional learning?

What additional activities will I incorporate?

Strategy 8

Metaphors, Analogies, and Similes

WHAT: DEFINING THE STRATEGY

The brain is a chain since it has many links.

Amygdala : Emotion : : Hippocampus : Long-term Memory

The consistency of the brain is like tofu and Jell-O.

When teaching about the brain, or anything else for that matter, metaphor, analogy, and simile are some of the most powerful strategies available. One of the brain's primary jobs is to make meaning or to look for patterns and connections between what one already knows and new information that one is acquiring. Therefore, when any new concept you are teaching can be compared with one that your participants already know and understand, neural connections are formed. Suddenly the new learning makes a whole lot more sense!

Watch how easily adults grasp new concepts through the use of this strategy. For example, by the time I finish teaching part of a workshop on the physiology of the brain, participants have stood up and cupped their hands to resemble a three-pound brain, wiggled their fingers to simulate the corpus callosum (or the structure that joins left and right hemispheres together), raised their arms as metaphors for a neuron, tapped the palm of their hands to identify the cell body of the neuron, and run their hand down their arm to recognize the axon of the neuron. All of these comparisons ensure that participants understand and remember pertinent facts about the miracle known as the brain. And this strategy works! Once this physiology lesson ends, participants sit and write down all of the brain facts that they can recall from memory within 2 minutes. Almost everyone in the entire workshop writes for the entire time. It is amazing how much the brain can remember when role play is combined with the strategy of metaphor, analogy, and simile.

WHY: THEORETICAL FRAMEWORK

- When semantic transformations like metaphor and analogy are used to explain a concept, a clear indication of a coherent understanding of that concept is shown (Jensen, 2009a).
- The concept of metaphor uses something familiar to explain something unfamiliar and something tangible to explain something conceptual (Jones, 2008).
- Students increase their ability to comprehend and make pertinent connections when analogies are used to explain or clarify ideas (Gregory & Parry, 2006).
- Since the frame of reference can be shifted when one concept is used to explain something else, teachers can introduce new knowledge using metaphors and analogies (Caine, Caine, McClintic, & Klimek, 2009).
- Synectics, using analogies or metaphors to connect ideas to a concept, can be used to engage the brain in creatively linking new information to prior knowledge (Keeley, 2008).
- Metaphors abstract some of the qualities of one concept and apply them in a new context (Caine, Caine, McClintic, & Klimek, 2009).
- Creating metaphors and creating analogies are two of the four types of tasks that should be used when identifying similarities and developing knowledge (Marzano, 2007).
- Using metaphors is another way of incorporating the thinking skills of compare and contrast (Gregory, 2008).
- Teachers must make a deliberate attempt to use metaphors across the curriculum (Gardner, 1983).
- Most concepts can be understood only in relation to other concepts (Lakoff & Johnson, 1980).

HOW: PROFESSIONAL LEARNING ACTIVITIES

- To facilitate understanding, introduce a new concept in relation to a concept the participants already know. For example, when teaching the concept of what confidence can do to a student's brain, I use the analogy of what it can do to a base-ball player's brain. A player who gets one hit often has the confidence to get another hit in the same game. Often, that confidence extends to other consecutive games and the hits become a streak. If your participants understand that con-cept in baseball, they will understand how students' belief in their ability to do calculus will facilitate their class perfor-mance. After all, *success breeds success!*

- Have participants use their bodies to simulate other concepts you wish to teach. For example, have participants stand and clasp their hands together to simulate a three-pound brain. Teach the following facts about the brain by having partici-pants follow these directions:

  1. Wiggle your thumbs to simulate the brain's frontal lobe.

  2. Separate your hands into the left and right hemispheres of the brain.

  3. Shake your left hand to recall characteristics once believed to be associated with the left hemisphere, such as analyti-cal, organized, structured, mathematical, and logical.

  4. Shake your right hand to recall characteristics once believed to be associated with the right hemisphere, such as artistic, creative, musical, global, and intuitive.

  5. Clasp your hands together again to demonstrate that the two hemispheres shouldn't be considered separate because they talk to each other through the corpus callo-sum, a connective brain region demonstrated visually by your clasped fingers.

- Given the pattern a : b :: c : d (a is to b as c is to d), have par-ticipants create analogies that show how two sets of ideas or concepts are related. For example, frontal lobe : problem-solving : : cerebellum : rote memories.

- People who think metaphorically think at very high levels. Have participants write metaphors that symbolize their understanding of two unrelated concepts. Have them explain to a partner how the two concepts are related. For example, if a person writes the metaphor, *the brain is a computer,* then the explanation becomes that they both make many connec-tions and have ways to access long-term memories.

- When helping participants acquire content-area vocabulary, compare the new vocabulary word to a concept the participants already know. For example, when teaching the French word *rouge,* which means *red,* have participants relate the concept to the red makeup *rouge,* which some women place on their cheeks.

- When teaching a major concept, have participants brainstorm what the concept would look like if it came to fruition. For example, ask this question: *What would a brain-compatible classroom look like?* Participants could then list some of the following: *a positive climate, good relationships between teacher and students, student choice, high challenge but low stress, excitement about learning, students talking with one another about content, students moving to learn content, hands-on learning,* and so forth.

- If you really think about it, analogies can often be made between what you are teaching and what participants can identify with in real life. This technique enables people to more easily remember the content. For example, when playing a ball game in one of my workshops, the rules state that the ball must be tossed to another person who is standing at a distance, yet if the ball is dropped at any time, the game must begin again. People are often reluctant to throw the ball too far since they are afraid they will not be able to throw or catch it. However, after they gain confidence, they always catch the ball. When the game is finished, to show a relationship between the game and life and the importance of challenge for the brain, I use the following analogy: *How would you ever know that you could catch a ball from a distance if the only balls you have ever caught in real life have been handed to you?* Another way to say the same thing was given to me by a teacher in one of my workshops. He learned it this way: *No great sailor ever sailed through calm seas!* People must be willing to take risks if they are to grow. Participants relate to me that when they really think about it, this concept can be life changing!

- Use metaphors to compare two unrelated concepts by having participants fill in the following blanks:

   If _____ were a _____, it would be _____ because _____. For example, If *myelin* were a *foodstuff,* it would be *vegetable shortening* because *it is a fatty substance.*

REFLECTION AND APPLICATION

How will I incorporate *metaphors, analogies, and similes* into professional learning to engage participants' brains?

Which metaphor, analogy, and simile activities am I already incorporating into professional learning?

What additional activities will I incorporate?

<big>Strategy</big> 

Strategy 9

Mnemonic Devices

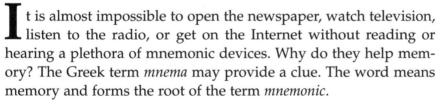

WHAT: DEFINING THE STRATEGY

PLC (Professional Learning Community)

RTI (Response to Intervention)

CCSS (Common Core State Standards)

SMART (Specific/Strategic, Measurable, Attainable, Results-oriented, Timebound) Goals

It is almost impossible to open the newspaper, watch television, listen to the radio, or get on the Internet without reading or hearing a plethora of mnemonic devices. Why do they help memory? The Greek term *mnema* may provide a clue. The word means memory and forms the root of the term *mnemonic*.

Out of all the professions, education is probably the one most replete with mnemonic devices (acronyms and acrostics). Everywhere I go, individual states and school systems have their own acronyms, or initials, for describing programs, tests, and concepts, and everyone in that system knows what those mean. They assume that I know them as well, which often I do not! *PLC, RTI,* and *SMART* are examples of mnemonic devices, which I refer to as *brain shortcuts*, methods that help the brain expedite the retention of pertinent information, since to remember the acronym is to provide a clue to the concept.

An acrostic is another type of mnemonic device and uses the principle of association. An acrostic is a sentence in which the first letter in each word stands for the first letter in the concept to be remembered. For example, to recall the spelling of the word *arithmetic*, one simply has to remember the sentence *A rat in the house may eat the ice cream.*

I use mnemonic devices whenever they are the appropriate strategy for assisting participants in retaining the information from a workshop or course. For example, the word *MENN (Meaning, Emotion, Need,* and *Novelty)* helps participants recall the four ways to gain the brain's attention since good-looking *men* can often attract the attention of others. What a difference it makes when we review content at the end! All I have to do is mention the acronym or acrostic and participants immediately recall the information.

WHY: THEORETICAL FRAMEWORK

- An acronym is a cue to help the brain retrieve information, since it tells the brain how many items should be remembered and "changes a recall task to an aided recall task" (Allen, 2008a, p. 16).
- Since mnemonic devices reduce large amounts of data into smaller sets or chunks, they can help people metacognitively encode and retrieve information (Materna, 2007).
- Acrostics work better if the original material is rather familiar, since students will still have to recall the original information from the trigger of the acrostic (Allen, 2008a).
- People who use mnemonics learn at least two to three times as much as those who learn through regular learning habits (Markowitz & Jensen, 2007).
- When used appropriately, mnemonic strategies involve higher-level thought processes, since they assist with the recall and understanding of information (Marzano, 2007).
- Acrostics are the most meaningful when the information has to be remembered in sequential order (Materna, 2007).
- When students are supplied with a mnemonic device, retention and recall are improved (Ronis, 2006).
- Ordinary people can greatly improve memory performance with mnemonic devices, since they are very useful for recalling unrelated patterns, information, or rules (Sousa, 2006).
- Since the human brain cannot retain more than an average of seven chunks of information in short-term memory simultaneously, mnemonics help to increase the amount of information in each chunk (Materna, 2007).
- The strategy of mnemonics has been used to improve memory in the professions of medicine and law enforcement, as well as in geriatric settings (Jensen & Dabney, 2000).

HOW: PROFESSIONAL LEARNING ACTIVITIES

- Education is probably the one profession that contains the largest number of mnemonic devices. There is an acronym for almost everything—PLC, RTI, SPED, IEP, MI, VAKT, and so forth. When teaching or putting information in writing, make certain that all participants know what the acronyms stand for by spelling the terms out the first time they are used.

"Today's session will focus on PBLA or Performance Based Learning Assessment, LASW or Looking At Student Work, TIO or Technology Integration Opportunities, and BFR or Break For Refreshments."

- Create acronyms to assist participants in recalling the most important information during a professional development opportunity. For example, I use the formula *AS = age* to help participants remember that a student's *attention span* in minutes is approximately equal to his or her age. Therefore, the attention span for a 12-year-old is 12 minutes. However, the bad news is that the attention span of a 90-year-old is not 90 minutes. The average attention span of the adult brain is approximately 20 minutes. There is an exception. When people are actively engaged and enjoying what they are doing, that formula seems obsolete. This is why a person can sit through a 2-hour movie and seldom move.

- Have participants work individually or in cooperative groups to create their own acronyms, which will assist them in recalling course content. For example, when I teach the four ways to gain the brain's attention—need, novelty, meaning, and emotion—I use the acronym N2aME. One teacher told me that the acronym N2aME would not get her attention, but two men (MEN2) certainly could. Another participant told me that when he sees two pretty women, he says the word AMEN2 twice. It is far better for participants to create their own acronyms than for you to give them some.

- Have participants create their own acrostics to help them remember information that may be difficult to recall. For example, to recall the original Southern colonies when teaching social studies teachers, I tell them the story of being a very good cook from the southern state of Georgia. Then I teach them the acrostic, **Very Nice Southerners Make Gravy!** which stands for **Virginia, North Carolina, South Carolina, Maryland,** and **Georgia.** A teacher thought up her own acrostic for the original middle colonies. It was No Dog, No Poop! which stands for New York, Delaware, New Jersey, and Pennsylvania.

- To recall the seven categories of Learning Forward's professional learning standards, Hayes Mizell, professor emeritus, suggests the following acronym. Chunk, or group, the three that begin with the letter L together. They are Learning Communities, Leadership, and Learning Designs. Then use the word DIRO to recall the four others. They are Documentation, Implementation, Resources, and Outcomes.

- Have participants create slogans or phrases to help them understand and remember important concepts. For example, when I teach classroom management, I teach students the following:

If your students like you, there is nothing they will not do for you. If your students don't like you, there is nothing they will not do to you.

- During the process of strategic planning, most schools and school districts have written mission statements that summarize what they are about. However, the mission statement is often too long to be memorized by all of the stakeholders. Therefore, a shorter phrase or sentence is used as the rallying point and is kept at the forefront of all decisions and memorized by all constituents. For example, the phrase *Students first!* would exemplify that everything done in the school district should be done in the best interest of students.

- Have participants use a peg-word system to link and recall items in a particular sequence. Have them think of a rhyming word for the numbers 1 through 10. For example, 1 = sun, 2 = shoe, 3 = bee, 4 = door, 5 = hive, 6 = sticks, 7 = heaven, 8 = gate, 9 = line, and 10 = men. Then have them associate each item on the list with the rhyming word in the weirdest visualization possible. For example, if the sixth item in a series of brain functions to be recalled is the cerebellum, have participants visualize the cerebellum being picked up by several sticks.

REFLECTION AND APPLICATION

How will I incorporate *mnemonic devices*
into professional learning to engage participants' brains?

*Which mnemonic devices am I already incorporating into my
professional learning?*

What additional devices will I incorporate?

Strategy 10

Movement

WHAT: DEFINING THE STRATEGY

Ateacher in a recent workshop walked up to me at the first break and related this story. She had forgotten to take her medication for her attention deficit hyperactivity disorder before coming to the workshop. However, she wanted to tell me that it didn't make a bit of difference since I had kept her and the rest of the class so actively engaged that she did not really need it! Most of your participants will not have this formal diagnosis, but they will still need the power of movement. How often have you attended a professional learning experience at which you sat, and sat, and sat, and sat, and the only person moving was your presenter? Compare what you learned and remembered from that workshop with what you learned from one in which you were actively engaged. There is actually no comparison!

Movement is one of the most important strategies on the list of 20 for engaging the adult brain. Anything learned while moving goes into one of the strongest memory systems in the brain—namely, procedural or muscle memory. This is why adults rarely forget how to drive a car (even one with a manual transmission), ride a bike, type, or play the piano. In fact, a teacher in another one of my classes related that her mother has Alzheimer's disease and no longer recognizes her children or grandchildren. However, her mother is a pianist and can still sit at the piano and remember how to play songs that she once played. You see, her fingers were moving across the piano keys when she originally learned to play the songs, and she has practiced them over the years, so they are housed in a strong memory system—procedural or muscle memory.

WHY: THEORETICAL FRAMEWORK

• Physical activity increases the brain's oxygen and glucose and, therefore, stimulates brain cells to connect to and talk with other brain cells (Materna, 2007).

• Prolonged aerobic exercise not only facilitates brain function and memory but also establishes an environment in which brand new brain cells can thrive (Lengel & Kuczala, 2010).

• Physical activity causes glycogen (glucose stored in the liver) to be released, which supports the formation of memories (Jensen, 2009b).

• Seventeen separate action research projects relate that using movement during learning can ready the brain and body for learning, increase the level of motivation, create a positive state for learning, increase the level of participation and engagement, and help people remember and recall information (Lengel & Kuczala, 2010).

• One important study showed that aerobic exercise can be as beneficial in treating depression as antidepressants (Ratey, 2008).

• When adults participated in a regular aerobic exercise program, short-term memory and creativity improved (Markowitz & Jensen, 2007).

• The presence or absence of a sedentary lifestyle was one of the greatest predictors of successful aging (Medina, 2008).

• Just as the senses of smell, taste, and sight trigger memory, so does movement (Markowitz & Jensen, 2007).

• Physical movement strengthens many more neurons than does the sedentary experience of a lecture (Jensen, 2007).

• People with an active lifestyle are more likely to live into their 90s, since exercise reduces the risk of heart attack or stroke by improving cardiovascular fitness (Medina, 2008).

• Physical performance is probably the only known cognitive activity that uses 100% of the brain (Jensen, 2008).

• Physical exercise increases two of the brain's neurotransmitters, dopamine and norepinephrine, which help to create a stable mood and assist in the transfer of information from short- to long-term memory (Khalsa, 1997).

HOW: PROFESSIONAL LEARNING ACTIVITIES

• Have participants draw the following clock on a sheet of paper. This clock will serve as the vehicle by which adults will make dates with other adults in your course or workshop. In fact, to add a little humor, I tell participants that after today, they can truthfully tell people that they had more than one date in the same day. Put on fast-paced music and have participants walk around the classroom, asking four people for dates and writing their names on the lines near each time. At appropriate times during the class, have participants keep each date by discussing a major concept or reteaching content. In a half-day workshop, participants usually keep a maximum of two dates. In a full day, three or four dates may be kept, or the clock dates can be used for more than one day.

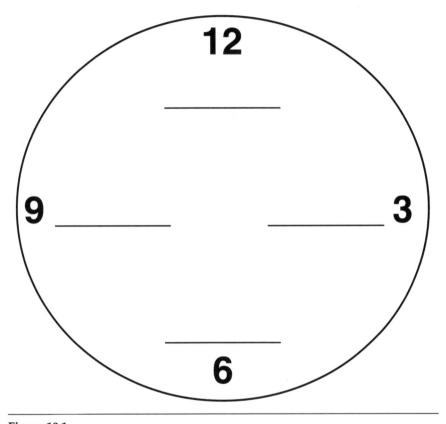

Figure 10.1

- Have participants draw the seasonal cycle below. Put on some fast-paced music and have them walk around the room making appointments with one participant for each season. Have them write the name of each participant on the appropriate line. When it becomes necessary for one peer to talk to another regarding something that is being taught in class or to reteach a concept previously taught, have them keep one of their four seasonal appointments. One seasonal cycle may last for 1 day or several days depending on how often participants need to talk and move simultaneously.

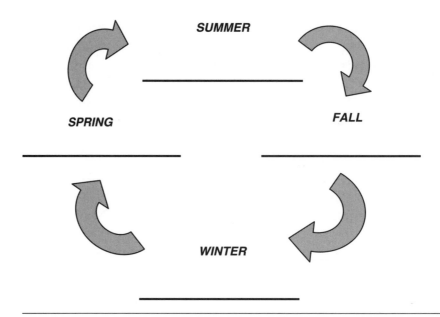

Figure 10.2

- Have participants gaze around the room until they lock eyes with someone who can be their energizing partner. They should be participants who are not sitting close by so that other participants have to get up to talk to them. Partners are given multiple opportunities to stand and talk with one another, to discuss an assigned topic, or to reteach a concept previously taught.
- When it is necessary for participants to read short passages aloud, have them stand and read. Standing supplies 5 to 15% more blood and oxygen throughout the body. Some of that will hopefully make its way to the brain and keep your participants more alert, especially in the afternoon after lunch.
- When a participant gives an answer to a question, have other participants stand if they agree with the original answer and remain seated if they disagree.
- When content needs to be reviewed, have participants stand and move around the room to the beat of some fast-paced, high-energy music. (Refer to *Strategy 11: Music, Rhythm, Rhyme, and Rap* for suggestions of high-energy types of music.) Stop the music and have participants form groups of four to six. Have them talk together with their group while standing for the purpose of answering a designated question or reviewing specific content together. Then start the music

again and repeat the process one or two additional times with new groups and new questions. Then have participants move or dance their way back to their original seats, invigorated and energized.

- Following a dialogue in which two opposing viewpoints are outlined, have participants move to the designated side of the room that corresponds to their point of view. For example, in an instructional methodology class, participants who support block scheduling move to the right side of the room; those who prefer traditional scheduling move to the left side of the room. Discussion ensues.

- Prepare a People Search by listing 12 incomplete statements regarding pertinent course content to be taught or reviewed in a 3 × 4 matrix on a piece of paper. Give each participant a copy of the matrix. While high-energy, fast-paced music is played, have participants circulate around the room finding others who can complete each statement. A different person must respond to each statement by providing the answer and initialing beside the answer for verification. The goal is for each person to have 12 different participants provide an answer to each statement before the song ends or before the allotted time is over.

- Involve participants in a Carousel Activity by writing one major topic to be reviewed on each of four posters and placing them at four different locations in the room. For example, if you are teaching a course on *Habit 7: Sharpen the Saw* of the *7 Habits of Highly Effective People*, your posters could relate to the four ways in which people need to restore themselves. Poster 1 would be *Mental,* Poster 2 would be *Physical,* Poster 3 would be *Social/Emotional,* and Poster 4 would be *Spiritual.* Divide participants into four groups. Have each group move to a different poster, then appoint a recorder, who is given a marker and writes the responses of the group on the poster. Then provide each group with 2 minutes to brainstorm as many things as they can to address the topic on the poster. When the 2 minutes are over and responses have been recorded, have each group move clockwise to the next poster and, within 2 minutes, add to the content already written. Carousel concludes when each group has had an opportunity to respond to each poster.

- Have participants visualize a continuum along one wall of the classroom to elicit participants' opinions regarding a related topic. The left-hand corner of the wall would represent 1 on the continuum and the right-hand corner of the wall would represent 10; therefore, the middle of the wall would correspond to 5. For example, during a trust-building workshop, have participants stand and go to a spot on the wall that represents the level of trust they have in the following groups of people: used-car salespeople, police officers, politicians, lawyers, teachers, administrators, or parents. Guide participants in a discussion of why they selected the spot that they did along the continuum.

REFLECTION AND APPLICATION

How will I incorporate *movement* into
professional learning to engage participants' brains?

Which movement activities am I already incorporating into my professional learning?

What additional activities will I incorporate?

Strategy 11

Music, Rhythm, Rhyme, and Rap

WHAT: DEFINING THE STRATEGY

Music soothes the savage beast—and the adult learner. The use of music can have a profound effect on the mood of your participants. If you want your teachers' brains calm, play classical, New Age, or jazz music as they enter your workshop. Calming music can reduce the stress level and remove the tired feeling that some teachers come in with, particularly if their professional learning opportunity is at the end of the school day. The number of beats in most of these selections ranges between 50 and 70 beats per minute. The heartbeat is within that range, so these types of music actually line up with the beat of the heart and calm down most brains.

If you want teachers motivated or if there is a need to celebrate a successful school experience, such as increases in test score results, use music with a faster tempo, such as salsa music, rhythm and blues, or fast-paced country. By the way, do you know what you get if you play a country song backwards? You get your house back, you get your job back, you get your wife back, and so forth!

I use music with a faster tempo, such as "Welcome Back Kotter" by John Sebastian, to invite participants to come back to class on time after breaks or lunch. When we need to review content following the teaching of a chunk of information, I use even faster music such as "Walking in Rhythm" by Donald Byrd as participants walk around the classroom, stop, and review what was learned with peers. At the end of class, we celebrate by moving to the left and right to "Celebrate" by Kool and the Gang so that every participant leaves class with such a positive feeling that they are willing to implement whatever was acquired during the professional learning experience.

WHY: THEORETICAL FRAMEWORK

- Music can lead to the following behavioral changes: establish the tone for the day, develop rapport with the audience, increase the energy level, align groups, create relaxation, stimulate and focus creativity, facilitate fun, and inspire the group (Jensen, 2009b).
- Teachers should use music to set a mood in the classroom, change the state of brains, and create a positive learning environment (Perez, 2008).
- Music has been shown to have the following potential effects on the mind and body: increase molecular and muscular energy, reduce pain and stress, speed up the healing and recovery process; help people release emotions; and increase creativity, thinking, and sensitivity (Jensen, 2008).
- Classical music by composers like Beethoven or Mozart cause beta waves to be stimulated in the brain and is appropriate to use when problem solving or brainstorming ideas (Sprenger, 2007).
- The type of music should be matched to the teachable tasks. For example, classical music from the baroque period or mellow New Age music can be used during seat work, rhythm and blues (R&B) for fun times, high-tempo for fast-paced movement, upbeat New Age for conversational work, oldies for sing-alongs or to accomplish tasks, or appropriate themes from television shows such as the theme from *Jeopardy* when playing the game (Jensen, 2009b).
- Music is considered brain based since there are many areas in the human brain that respond specifically to music (Jensen, 2005).
- Change the music during a learning episode. Select emotional music to help you set a mood before class starts, upbeat tunes for when participants are moving around the room, appropriate music during seatwork, and positive music for the end of class (Sousa, 2006).
- The musical arts have the ability to engage all people, since they can break down barriers between religions, cultures, races, geographic distinctions, and socioeconomic statuses (Jensen, 2005).
- The brain seems to be specialized for music, since brain cells process the contour of the melody and the auditory cortex responds to tones and pitch (Weinberger, 2004).
- Music activates different parts of the brain depending on the learning task. For example, harmony and rhythm activate more of the left brain and melody activates more of the right brain, while the cerebellum is activated by measuring beats (Jensen, 2008).
- Learning to play a musical instrument or the love of music is one of the 10 things that keep people living above the age of 80 (Mahoney, 2005).

HOW: PROFESSIONAL LEARNING ACTIVITIES

- Buy an iPod, which will make the inclusion of music in your presentation so much easier. iPods enable you to download music and arrange it by artist, album, or song. You can also make separate playlists for the different workshops or courses that you teach. Then buy a sound dock that will enable you to broadcast your music to your audience. I use a Bose Wave Sound Dock, which has impeccable sound and, if charged at night, will play 6 hours of music without a connection to electricity. This enables you to place your music anywhere in the teaching environment.

- Play appropriate calming music as participants enter your classroom. Types of music that fall into this category include classical, smooth jazz, New Age, slow Celtic, Native American, and nature sounds. Calming music will also help to establish a supportive environment and assist participants in relaxing and readying themselves for the upcoming instruction.

- Incorporate specific music that is appropriate for the concepts you are teaching. For example, when it is time for participants to talk with one another, play "Let's Give Them Something to Talk About" by Bonnie Raitt. When I am teaching about how humor can put the brain in a positive state and strengthen memory, I play "Don't Worry, Be Happy" by Bobby McFerrin.

- Play fast-paced, high-energy music whenever you want to energize your audience and increase their state of arousal. Music in this category includes salsa, R&B, rock and roll, fast-paced country, positive rap, and big-band sounds. Since the number of beats per minute falls in the range of 110 to 160, this type of music is particularly helpful following lunch or in the late afternoon, when people are more likely to become lethargic.

HOW TO DELIVER MEMORABLE STAFF DEVELOPMENT

A.BACALL

"I need three teachers to come up here and sing backup."

- Play baroque music during a class review to assist participants in remembering the concepts taught.
- At the end of breaks and/or lunch, let music bring participants back to your class. Select and play music that tells the class that it is time for instruction to resume. Such songs could include "Welcome Back, Kotter" by John Sebastian, "Baby Come Back" by Player, "Does Anyone Really Know What Time It Is?" by Chicago, or "Time in a Bottle" by Jim Croce. When the song ends, participants should be in their seats ready to learn. As an added bonus, if my adult audience gets back to their seats by the end of the song, I tell them a joke.
- After teaching a major concept, have participants work with a partner or in small groups to write a song, rhyme, or rap that shows that they have understood the concept.
- Following the teaching of a major concept, have participants work with a partner or in small groups to create a cinquain that shows what they have learned. A cinquain's format is as follows: first line, one word; second line, two words; third line, three words; fourth line, four words; last line, one word. Example:

  Learning

  Growing dendrites

  Making numerous connections

  Celebrations in the brain

  Thinking

- Music can change the state of the adult brain. Consult books that can assist you with your selection of music, such as Eric Jensen's (2005) *Top Tunes for Teaching* or Rich Allen's (2008b) *The Ultimate Book of Music for Learning.*
- Listed below are just a few of my favorite genres of music and artists that I have on my iPod. I play these selections when I want to change the state of my adult or student learners' brains.

MUSIC FOR THE BRAIN

Calming

Easy Rock Volume 1
The Best Relaxing Classics

The Most Relaxing Classical Album in the World...Ever! (Disc 1)
The Most Relaxing Classical Album, Vol. 2 (Disc 1)
The Most Relaxing New Age Music in the Universe
Stardust—The Great American Songbook (Rod Stewart)
Sydney Aquarium
Tribute to Enya

Emile Pandolfi—Classical Pianist

An Affair to Remember
By Request
Days of Wine and Roses
Secret Love
Some Enchanted Evening

Jazz

The Best Smooth Jazz...Ever! (Disc 1)
Body Language (Boney James)
Ultimate Kenny G
At Last—The Duets Album (Kenny G)
The Greatest Hits of All (George Benson)
Best of Hiroshima

Other Artists' Greatest Hits

The Very Best of Acoustic Alchemy
Sounds of Summer (The Beach Boys)
The Very Best of the Bee Gees
Best of the Doobies
Earth, Wind, and Fire—Greatest Hits
The Emotions: Super Hits
The Hits (Faith Hill)
Greatest Hits (Gloria Estefan)
The Very Best of Kool & the Gang
Motown Classics
The Ultimate Collection (Michael McDonald)
Hits (Phil Collins)
The Best of Carlos Santana
Song Review: A Greatest Hits Collection (Stevie Wonder)

REFLECTION AND APPLICATION

> How will I incorporate *music, rhythm, rhyme, and rap* into professional learning to engage participants' brains?

Which music, rhythm, rhyme, and rap activities am I already incorporating into my professional learning?

What additional activities will I incorporate?

Strategy 12

Project-Based and Problem-Based Instruction

WHAT: DEFINING THE STRATEGY

Neuroscientists have found that throughout history, those characteristics that did not enhance the brain and body's survival in the real world have disappeared, while those attributes that enhanced survival have endured or become more pronounced over time (Westwater & Wolfe, 2000). Is it any wonder, then, that, according to adult learning theory, professional learning opportunities that are directed at solving specific, real-world, job-related challenges are the most effective for making lasting behavior change (Collins, 2000; Snyder, 1993)? This is why it makes so much sense for schools to become professional learning communities. In fact, the problems or challenges encountered when schools are attempting to increase student achievement form the basis of the work of the PLCs.

I teach 10 different courses, and they receive rave reviews! However, not until I integrated a real-world project into each class did I expect that the information from the workshop would be carried over into the classroom. For example, in one class, following the playing of a review game, we list 10 characteristics of a brain-compatible classroom. Some of those characteristics include a positive environment, music, visuals, students talking about content, and students moving to learn content. The follow-up project is to pick 2 of those 10 characteristics to implement in the classroom.

Participants must practice those characteristics for a minimum of 21 days or 28 times, whichever comes first, since that is the minimum amount of time it will take to make the two characteristics habits in their teaching. Will every teacher actually complete the project? Probably not! But if someone, such as an administrator or mentor, continues to follow up on the project, the likelihood that it will be done increases.

WHY: THEORETICAL FRAMEWORK

- Successful professional learning communities work to develop a clear purpose and a focus on problems of practice (Wiedrick, 2011).
- "The more complex the problem, the more complex the brain activity becomes" (Fogarty, 2009, p. 154).
- Problem solving can be supported during adult learning by incorporating movement, interaction, and the creation of products (Gregory & Kuzmich, 2007).
- Effective professional learning communities observe, problem solve, support and give advice to, teach, and learn from one another (Wiedrick, 2011).
- Project-based instruction provides the brain with the intrinsic rewards of natural curiosity and a search for meaning (Ronis, 2006).
- There is no limit to the number, type, and scope of projects that can be used at the beginning or culmination of a unit of study (Fogarty, 2009).
- Adults experience empowerment and purpose when they create or locate solutions to problems that make a difference to them (Gregory & Kuzmich, 2007).
- Parallel processing occurs in the brain when the brain is making decisions or problem solving (Fogarty, 2001).
- People need opportunities to interact within the larger context of conflicting situations and solving real-world problems (Caine, Caine, McClintic, & Klimek, 2009).

HOW: PROFESSIONAL LEARNING ACTIVITIES

- Following a workshop or course segment, assign a follow-up project through which participants can implement the concepts learned during instruction. For example, when I teach the TESA (Teacher Expectations and Student Achievement) class, participants must pick 3 of the 15 TESA interactions to implement in their classrooms over the next 21 days or 28 times. They also pair with another teacher in the course who observes them for the interactions chosen.

- Have participants work individually, with grade levels, or with departments to solve a real-world, job-embedded problem. Have them identify the problem, brainstorm possible solutions, research the feasibility of those solutions, and select one or more for possible implementation. Once implemented, the effectiveness of the solutions should be assessed.

- Have participants work with grade levels or departments to analyze both norm- and criterion-referenced test data for grade levels or individual students. Have them make decisions regarding student strengths and areas in need of improvement. Grade-level or departmental plans are formulated based on what the data show.

- Have participants analyze student work, such as written compositions or mathematics word problems, for the purpose of identifying mastery and areas in need of improvement. Have them share their observations with students, who can also contribute to the conversations around their individual performances.

- Have participants participate in a project in which they videotape and analyze a lesson segment of their teaching. Then, individually or with colleagues, have them analyze the strengths and areas for enhancement, setting SMART (Specific/Strategic, Measurable, Attainable, Results-oriented, Timebound) goals to be accomplished.

- Involve participants in a project in which they develop a teaching portfolio that showcases artifacts indicative of professional growth. These could include, but are not limited to, evidence of increases in student achievement, commendations from parents, video clips of lessons taught, additional extracurricular responsibilities, and so forth.

REFLECTION AND APPLICATION

How will I incorporate *project-based and problem-based instruction* into professional learning to engage participants' brains?

Which project-based and problem-based instructional activities am I already incorporating into my professional learning?

What additional activities will I incorporate?

Strategy **13**

Reciprocal Teaching, Cooperative Learning, and Peer Coaching

WHAT: DEFINING THE STRATEGY

When I facilitate the workshop *Worksheets Don't Grow Dendrites*, the participants' first major activity is to individually write down as many facts as they can recall following my brain-compatible biology lesson. Since the brain likes challenge, the objective is to recall at least 12 facts about the brain. Very few participants are able to recall that many facts working alone. Then participants work with their first date, or appointment, and are given additional time to share what they have written and find out what their partner has written with the goal of having at least 12 combined facts about the brain. By the time participants have worked together, almost everyone in class has met the objective, and the majority of the class will even receive extra credit for having at least 15 facts about the brain. You see, *two heads are better than one!*

Very little is done in the adult world of work by oneself. Most tasks are accomplished by a team of people. However, when I was taught to teach over 40 years ago, if two students were talking about the content together, they were accused of cheating. Now that same activity is called cooperative learning. In fact, the brain research is telling us that the brain learns at least 95% of what it is able to teach to someone else.

Here is another example. My daughter, Jennifer, teaches some of the same courses that I do. To prepare for this arduous task, she shadowed me for several summers, learning the content of the workshops. When she was ready, I began to have her reteach to me in the hotel room at night what I was teaching during the day, realizing that if she could teach me what she knew, she could teach anyone else. She no longer needs my guidance, since she gets rave reviews for her ability to teach the content in a masterful way. It makes me wonder! Shouldn't the job of any teacher be to get students to the point where they no longer need you? If fact, our job should be to do ourselves out of a job. But not to worry! There will always be other students and adults who need our expertise!

WHY: THEORETICAL FRAMEWORK

- Healthy human brains are wired to connect and to be social. For example, mirror neurons in the brain are activated when we see another person engage in an act, such as eating (Hyerle & Alper, 2011).
- The capability to work with other people is one of the most essential and marketable skills that a teacher can give to students (Tileston, 2011).
- Possible team structures that encourage collaboration include the following: (1) same-course or grade-level teams; (2) vertical teams that link teachers with others who teach students above and below their grade level; (3) electronic teams that technologically link teachers with peers across the district, state, or world; (4) interdisciplinary teams in which multiple content-area teachers work interdependently for a curricular goal; and (5) logical links where physical education or music teachers join a grade level team to accomplish a mutual outcome (Dufour et al., 2010).
- The *"cooperative* or *collaborative family"* of a school produces collective energy that increases positive affect and the learning and implementation of knowledge and skills (Joyce & Calhoun, 2010, p. 64).
- American teachers spend less time than their counterparts in other nations planning and learning together about high-quality instruction and curriculum (Darling-Hammond et al., 2009).
- When teachers supported themselves through peer-coaching groups that met regularly together and planned and discussed lessons, implementation rates of new knowledge and skill exceeded 90% (Joyce & Calhoun, 2010).
- Quality teaching is not an individual accomplishment. It is the result of a collaborative culture that empowers teachers to team up to improve student learning beyond what any one of them can achieve alone (Carroll, 2009).
- High-performing, high-poverty schools have structures in place to ensure that teachers work together rather than in isolation for the purpose of improving instruction and making sure that every student is learning (Chenoweth, 2009).
- It is imperative that professional learning be directed at improving the quality of collaborative work (National Staff Development Council, 2006).
- People remember 95% of what they teach to someone else (Glasser, 1990).

HOW: PROFESSIONAL LEARNING ACTIVITIES

- When participants need to reteach a concept just taught or provide a summary of the key points in a class discussion, have them turn to their close partner (CP) or someone who is sitting so close to them that they do not have to get up to talk with them. Give these close partners a name. They can be Ducks or Geese, Partners A and B, or X and Y Variables in a math class.

- Sometimes, as a change of pace or if you have an uneven number of people at a table, you will want participants to work in trios. Their names can be Lions, Tigers, and Bears (Oh My!); Duck, Duck, Goose; or X, Y, and Z Variables.

- Divide your class into groups, or families, of four to six. The word *families* satisfies the brain's basic need to belong. Typically, a family will occupy one table in a workshop or course. When a topic or question needs to be discussed, having *families* talk to one another works perfectly. They provide opportunities for more participants to talk simultaneously than would a whole-class discussion. I also tell participants that if they have a question or need something re-explained, to ask their close partner first and then turn to a family member if the explanation is not sufficient. If there is still no resolution, then they should ask me, their teacher.

"Let's break up into small groups and come to a joint resolution."

- Have participants work in pairs to interview one another regarding a professional article or book that each has read. Then have participants report on their partner's book to the entire class, or in small groups if the class is too large.

- To create the concept of positive interdependence, or participants relying on one another in a group, have them assume roles to expedite the group's functioning. These roles could include, but are not limited to, the following:

- o *Presenter or Facilitator:* Presents group findings to the class
- o *Recorder:* Writes down group ideas or answers
- o *Timekeeper:* Informs the group when half the time is over and when there is one minute remaining
- o *Resource Manager:* Collects the materials that the group needs to complete the task
- o *Encourager:* Encourages each participant to contribute to the discussion and praises them when they do
- o *Observer:* Informs participants of how well they are practicing the social skills previously taught
- Have participants work in pairs or small groups to compare answers on a homework assignment, discuss any disparities, correct their papers, and provide a written explanation of why an answer might need to be changed.
- Following the completion of a cooperative group activity, have each group appoint a *roving reporter*, whose job it is to travel in a clockwise fashion to other groups and report the results of the original group's work.
- Following a workshop or course in which new knowledge or skills have been acquired, assign each teacher a peer (or have them select one) who can provide assistance and support as the new behavior is implemented. For example, when the TESA (Teacher Expectations and Student Achievement) Program is taught, teachers pair with their peers and observe and support one another as they implement the 15 interactions learned in the workshop.
- Assign a well-qualified, veteran teacher who can serve as a mentor to a less-experienced peer. Mentors should possess the following qualifications and personal characteristics:
  - o an understanding of academic standards
  - o sensitivity to teacher concerns
  - o the ability to transmit effective teaching strategies
  - o the ability to listen and communicate openly
  - o an understanding of diverse teaching styles
  - o restraint from judgment
  - o ability to model continuous learning
- According to Jo Ellen Killion (2009), there are 10 major roles that coaches should assume. They are as follows:
  1. Data coach—assisting teachers in examining student data for the purpose of designing instruction
  2. Resource provider—accessing supplies, books, lesson or unit plans, guest speakers for teachers

3. Mentor—acclimating new teachers to the school's professional norms, practices, and policies

4. Curriculum specialist—deepening teachers' understanding of what concepts they should be teaching

5. Instructional specialist—helping teachers select appropriate methodologies and differentiate instruction to meet students' needs

6. Classroom supporter—working inside the classroom to model effective teaching practices

7. Learning facilitator—organizing, designing, supporting, and facilitating learning that enhances or deepens teachers' understanding of instructional practices or content knowledge

8. School leader—leading reform efforts within their schools and assisting teachers in implementing those reforms

9. Catalyst for change—serving as a change agent who helps teachers abandon stagnant practice and analyze and reflect on what they are doing

10. Learner—engaging in continuous professional development (such as conferences and workshops) to strengthen personal coaching skills

    • Provide participants desirous of becoming administrators with the opportunity to shadow an effective veteran administrator. The participant follows the administrator and experiences the day's events. After the observation, a discussion ensues regarding the situations observed and the ways in which they were handled.

REFLECTION AND APPLICATION

How will I incorporate *reciprocal teaching, cooperative learning, and peer coaching* into professional learning to engage participants' brains?

Which reciprocal teaching, cooperative learning, and peer coaching activities am I already incorporating into my professional learning?

What additional activities will I incorporate?

Strategy 14

Role Plays, Drama, Pantomimes, and Charades

WHAT: DEFINING THE STRATEGY

Have you ever attended an adult party at which a spirited game of Charades was the order of the day? If so, then you realize how involved adults can get when acting out words or phrases that their team members are attempting to guess. Your adult participants can get just that energetic when you are asking them to role play as well. The strategy of role play places the body as close to the actual event as possible without them having to be there.

I still remember when I was in graduate school taking a course in which the topic was principle-centered leadership, a subject outlined in Stephen Covey's book by the same name. One of the activities that our professor, Dr. Tucker, had us engaged in was a television interview. We had to pretend that we were conducting an interview with Covey himself and design a series of questions that we would ask him related to his work. Then we had to actually answer the questions as if we were Stephen Covey. This meant taking what we had read and applying it in a practical context, which required a higher level of thought than just writing a paper outlining the salient points in the book.

At the next class session, we took turns pretending to be either the moderator or Stephen Covey during an in-depth interview in which we either asked or answered designated questions from Covey's point of view. Why do I still remember this night of class when I don't remember many of the other ones? It was because of the use of role play to get across the content. Dr. Tucker could have lectured us on Covey's work, but it would not have been nearly as memorable.

WHY: THEORETICAL FRAMEWORK

• Role playing makes accommodations for multiple perspectives and can be very powerful for engaging learners of all ages (Ginsberg, 2011).
• Physical performance is probably the only known cognitive activity that uses 100% of the brain (Jensen, 2008).
• The main goal of role play is to create an experience that is as realistic as possible, since it engages the intellect, emotions, and physical senses (Ginsberg, 2011).
• Since our knowledge is dependent on the state of the brain, things that are learned during role play may be accessible later on should that same situation occur (Jensen, 2008).
• Having groups practice summarizing, clarifying, and probing in role-play situations is much more impactful than simply telling adults how important those skills are (Nash, 2010).
• Role playing is applicable to all subject areas and takes into consideration multiple perspectives (Ginsberg, 2011).
• During simulations, learning is more enjoyable and memorable, since more creativity and choice are utilized and there is little fear of negative evaluation (Jensen, 2008).
• When people act out a concept, the memory of that concept is stored not only in the mind but in the body as well (Jensen, 2007).
• Role plays use spatial, visual, linguistic, and bodily modalities, and, therefore, not only access emotions but also enable the brain to comprehend at much deeper levels than a lecture would (Gregory & Parry, 2006).
• The more closely a role-play activity imitates the psychological and physiological states the brain enters when applying the information in real life, the easier it is to retrieve the memory of the learning when trying to recall it later (Jensen, 2007).
• Simulations increase meaning, are highly motivating, and facilitate transfer of knowledge (Wolfe, 2001).

HOW: PROFESSIONAL LEARNING ACTIVITIES

• A presenter loses his or her credibility very quickly when he or she tells teachers that they should actively engage students during instruction and then that same presenter shows multiple PowerPoint slides while failing to actively engage the audience. Teachers are expecting you to walk the talk! When I teach any workshop, regardless of the content, I model or role play the 20 brain-compatible strategies that I write about in my books and that I expect every teacher to consistently use. Teachers tell me that the modeling during the workshop is what convinces them to give the 20 strategies a try with their students.

- Have participants use their bodies to become the concept being taught. For example, when teaching the physiology of the brain, have participants stand and fold their hands together to resemble a three-pound brain. Have them wiggle their thumbs to simulate the frontal lobe, where much of the higher-level thinking occurs, separate their hands into fists resembling left and right hemispheres, and wiggle their fingers to role play the function of the corpus callosum.

- Following the completion of a book study, turn your classroom into a talk show. Create a list of questions that would be asked of the book author if he or she were being interviewed. Have participants take turns being the author of the book and answering the questions as the author would. In this way, you can discern which important concepts have been understood.

- Give participants cards containing the names of concepts previously taught in class. Have participants take turns coming to the front of the class and acting out or pantomiming the assigned concepts while the rest of the class attempts to guess the name of the concept.

- Following a lecture or discussion on how to conduct an effective parent-teacher conference, have a teacher volunteer to come to the front of the room and role play a parent–teacher conference in which you are playing the role of the parent. Following a discussion of the conference, have participants work in pairs and take turns role playing their own conferences.

- Prior to contacting a student's family via a home visit, have teachers role play how to make the home visit effective, including respectful greetings, beginning the conversation with the family, deepening the conversation, asking appropriate questions, and concluding the visit (Ginsberg, 2011).

- During a course on effective teaching practices, have one participant model an effective lesson by teaching content to a few members of the class. For example, when I teach the course TESA (Teacher Expectations and Student Achievement), I ask one teacher to conduct a 5-minute lesson on any subject he or she chooses while modeling the three TESA interactions I have just taught. Participants observe and code the lesson by placing a tally mark on a sheet each time a TESA interaction is modeled in the lesson.

- To teach teachers how ineffective instruction can be, I role play the way I remember being taught social studies. I ask one group of teachers to pretend that they are in my social studies class and to open their imaginary books to page 5. Then I ask person number one to read the first paragraph aloud, person number two to read the second, and so forth. I ask the class, *What is person number five doing while person number one is reading paragraph one?* The answer is always *reading ahead to her or his paragraph.* This role play is used to demonstrate how ineffective round-robin oral reading can be when expecting students to pay attention. It takes many adults back to memories of their own social studies classrooms. Role play can work well to model the use of both effective and ineffective instructional strategies.

- One of the most meaningful responsibilities of the mentor or instructional coach is to go into the classroom of a teacher and model what an effective lesson should look like. As a consultant, I also provide model lessons regarding the use of the 20 brain-compatible strategies while other teachers observe the lesson. It is a win–win situation. Not only do I get to try out the strategies on the students of the teachers with whom I am working, but I also gain credibility from the teachers when they personally observe me teaching the same students they teach on a daily basis. When the lesson is over, the teachers and I go into another room and the following three questions guide our discussion:

1. Which of the 20 brain-compatible strategies did you see me use with the students?

2. What were the strengths of the lesson?

3. How could the lesson have been improved?

REFLECTION AND APPLICATION

> How will I incorporate *role plays, drama, pantomimes, and charades* into professional learning to engage participants' brains?

Which role plays, drama, pantomimes, and charades am I already incorporating into my professional learning?

What additional activities will I incorporate?

Strategy 15

Storytelling

WHAT: DEFINING THE STRATEGY

When I served as executive director of professional development for the DeKalb County School System, one of my most important jobs was to head a committee that planned and executed the Summer Leadership Conference for all of the administrators in the system. We attempted to make the conference so memorable that, although the participants didn't have to leave the school system, they would experience the highest quality of professional learning. We would bring in the most reputable national presenters we could find to address the topics that were in line with the school system's instructional and administrative priorities. Since the brain remembers first and last more easily than it recalls middle, I would always make sure that the opening and closing speakers were inspirational, motivational, and memorable.

One year, the opening speaker told an emotional story that moved the audience to tears as he held them in the palm of his hand. The closing speaker arrived 2 days later and had not been there during the initial session. Unfortunately, he told the very same story and did not understand why his speech did not have the same effect on the audience. The moral of this story is to tell your own stories—ones that have happened to you personally or to people you know personally.

The brain remembers a story for several reasons. It is connected with a beginning, a middle, and an end. It provides insight into the personality of the speaker and can make the content relevant to the audience. If the story happens to be emotional or humorous, its recall value is increased. The next time you are at a conference or any venue for an adult audience, watch how attentive the audience gets when the presenter tells a story.

WHY: THEORETICAL FRAMEWORK

- Telling stories is one of the oldest ways in the world to convey the ideals and values of a community (Dufour et al., 2010).
- Telling stories is one of the most powerful tools for shaping the feelings and thinking of others (Patterson, Grenny, Maxfield, McMillan, & Switzler, 2008).
- Good stories put a human face on success by providing role models that can clarify for others what is noted, appreciated, and valued (Dufour et al., 2010).
- Stories can be powerful learning tools, since they provide clarity, create lasting and powerful images in the mind, and help adults remember factual material (Nash, 2010).
- Good stories are more convincing and compelling than mere data alone, since they appeal to both the head and the heart (Dufour et al., 2010).
- The concrete images in stories activate emotions and sense of meaning and provide context and cues for new information (Markowitz & Jensen, 2007).
- Curriculum can be connected to a larger purpose through storytelling and the activities that follow the story (Caine, Caine, McClintic, & Klimek, 2009).
- Most things that are problems today become stories tomorrow (Delehant, 2007).
- Ancient cultures have used the tradition of storytelling for passing on memory from one generation to the next generation (Markowitz & Jensen, 2007).
- Since even young children acquire a sense of narrative, human beings naturally relate to stories (Caine, Caine, McClintic, & Klimek, 2009).
- Concrete images in stories activate our emotions and sense of meaning and supply cues and contexts for new information (Markowitz & Jensen, 2007).
- Proximity, silences, questioning, or storytelling enable strong leaders and good facilitators to redirect the group when times get challenging (Delehant, 2007).

HOW: PROFESSIONAL LEARNING ACTIVITIES

- Tell participants a story as the opening activity of a workshop or course. Because the brain remembers best what it hears first, your opening story will be long remembered. If the story is funny or emotional, its impact is increased. Remember to tell stories from your own personal experiences or from what others have shared with you personally and not ones that your audience is likely to have heard before. For example, the story "Three Letters from Teddy" is a tear-jerking story of a teacher who came to believe in a little boy others thought would not amount to anything but who became a doctor and asked that his teacher sit at his wedding where his deceased mother would have. The first time I heard that story, I cried all the way through. Now, when I hear it, I think, *Oh, here we go again!*

- Create and tell stories to participants throughout the workshop or course that teach pertinent concepts or ideas you want your class to remember. Never tell stories just for the sake of telling stories. Your time is too important for that, and so is their time!

- Have participants work individually or in small groups to create their own stories, which will help them recall events in sequential order or steps in a multistep process.

- Have participants tell their individual stories or give personal testimonies related to a concept being taught. For example, when teaching the TESA (Teacher Expectations and Student Achievement) course, before I teach the interaction of Praise, I ask for volunteers to tell about a time when a teacher did or said something so devastating that they still remember it to this day. The countless number of stories that participants still vividly recall, even if the stories took place when they were in kindergarten, would surprise you. Often, the emotion is still so great to the teacher that tears are shed during the telling. Then I ask volunteers to recall a time when a teacher did or said something so encouraging that they still remember it to this day. By the time participants have finished their personal stories, every person realizes the emotional impact a teacher can have on a student, either for good or for bad!

- During PLC meetings, have teachers share stories or anecdotal data about students being discussed. These true stories will go a long way toward helping teachers form a total picture of the student and can add much to the objective test data being considered.

- Every school faculty should know the story or history of the school in which they teach. The history should be recorded in writing and include rituals, events, and people who have made significant contributions to the school and its accomplishments. This story should be ongoing and will help new employees to the school understand the culture and climate of the current building. During strategic planning or other professional learning community opportunities, this history should be reviewed and remembered.

- One effective way to conclude your workshop or course is with a story. Remember that the brain remembers second-best what it hears last, so your culminating stories will be long remembered. Be certain that the story is illustrative of concepts you have taught and serves as a summary or reflection for your participants.

REFLECTION AND APPLICATION

How will I incorporate *storytelling* into
professional learning to engage participants' brains?

Which storytelling activities am I already incorporating into my professional learning?

What additional activities will I incorporate?

Strategy **16**

Technology

WHAT: DEFINING THE STRATEGY

My publisher, Corwin, approached me about the possibility of being one of their first authors to plan and implement an online course based on my books. My first inclination was to say, *Thanks, but no thanks!* since so many of the brain-based strategies I teach are grounded in face-to-face contact, such as cooperative learning or storytelling. However, the more I thought about it, the more I began to see the benefit in considering another medium for getting the message out to teachers that there are 20 ways to instruct the brains of students and adults. Well, I outlined the class, and the staff from PD360 did an excellent job of deciding the best technological format for displaying it. Before long, together we had in place a wonderful 10-hour course, called Growing Dendrites, that enables teachers from all over to interact technologically with other teachers, to view me and other teachers working directly with students, and to submit plans for integrating the 20 strategies into their daily lessons. I was even able to participate in a webinar while I was in Olathe, Kansas, the moderator was in Salt Lake City, Utah, and the teachers who participated were in Gardenia, California. Thus, the wonders of technology!

Professional learning in the 21st century brings online instruction, distance-learning telecasts, intercontinental e-mails, high-tech presentation tools, and myriad exceptional educational experiences. Just remember to balance the advantages of technological experiences with the irreplaceable face-to-face contact between teacher and students.

WHY: THEORETICAL FRAMEWORK

- Computer access, the Internet, interactive whiteboards, e-books, and online courses put a classroom in "first-class cyber position" (Feinstein & Kiner, 2011, p. 118).
- "Distance learning has the ability to ignite a wide-reaching revolution in the field of professional development" (Joyce & Calhoun, 2010, p. 12).
- Professional development training with the accompanying technology support helps to ensure that the classroom is "plugged in and wired" (Feinstein & Kiner, 2011, p. 118).
- An aging brain that can suffer from a reduction in cell activity, atrophy, and plaque growth can be helped when that brain is searching on the Internet (University of California–Los Angeles, 2009).
- Technology has the capability to increase learning, motivation, and collaboration and the ability to solve problems (Pitler, Hubbell, Kuhn, & Malenoski, 2007).
- Elder adults who use the Internet can stimulate and reshape their brains by simultaneously holding information in working memory longer while dealing with graphics and narratives (University of California–Los Angeles, 2009).
- Educators are now finding that blogs can improve writing skills, wikis foster collaboration, Skype engages people in discussion while not in the classroom, and niche group software enables people to create their own music (Brown, 2008).
- Technology enables schools to communicate with parents (often in several different languages) regarding pertinent school information, emergencies, school closings, and so forth (Lemmon, 2008).
- Technology assists school leaders in managing and integrating vital student achievement data (Paben, 2002).
- Online learning should be used to enhance face-to-face learning. There is no virtual learning miracle that will eradicate the need for people (Cookson, 2001).

HOW: PROFESSIONAL LEARNING ACTIVITIES

- Have participants complete some class assignments online and e-mail them to you by a designated period of time.
- Have participants follow the necessary requirements for enrolling in an online certification course or a master's, specialist's, or doctoral program and meet the necessary requirements for completion. The best programs of study include both online and face-to-face class sessions.
- Have participants go online to access websites replete with sample content standards, scope and sequence charts, curricular objectives, and sample lesson plans that can be incorporated into their individual planning. For example,

researchers at McREL (Mid-Continent Research for Education and Learning) have identified more than 200 standards and thousands of benchmarks in both state- and national-level documents for 14 different content areas.

- Have participants go on TeacherTube to access videos of sample teaching lessons and the use of music to teach content objectives.

- Have participants visit the classrooms of master teachers or confer with experts in a given field without ever leaving the building via distance-learning telecasts.

- Have participants use a computer program such as Test Tracks to compile, disaggregate, and analyze student achievement data. The resulting trends should assist in identifying strengths and areas in need of improvement that will be addressed during PLC meetings.

- Incorporate technology into your presentations through the use of presentation tools such as Microsoft PowerPoint. Limit the number of slides, since any tool, no matter how effective, loses its effectiveness when overused. (Refer to *Strategy 18: Visuals* for guidelines regarding the effective use of PowerPoint.) Provide participants with a miniature printout of the slides so that their attention can be focused on the ensuing discussion and not on copying the text from the slides.

"It's an unfortunate fact that teachers receive less professional development in technology than any other professional group. Please pay close attention as this will be the only staff development you will receive all year."

- A document camera or Elmo provides even more flexibility with your presentation, since anything you put under it your audience will be able to see, such as sample student written work, stories with pictures, and visuals that enhance your presentation.
- Encourage your participants to utilize technology throughout a course when making a presentation or completing a class assignment. Teachers who are digital natives will have no trouble easily doing so. Digital immigrants like myself, may need a little help from their students or children.
- Establish electronic learning teams that give participants opportunities to discuss pertinent issues, share experiences, or provide coaching to one another.
- Provide or have participants create online newsletters that reinforce course content or expand the learning.
- Provide appropriate software programs, such as SmartWeb or Gradebook, that will expedite an administrator's ability to schedule classes, maintain attendance and discipline records, calculate averages and compile grades, and e-mail pertinent information to parents. Professional learning classes in the use of these programs are integral to successful implementation.
- Make participants aware of the inappropriate use of Facebook and other social networks. Having students as online friends or posting unprofessional pictures on personal Facebook sites can lead to censure and possible termination from a teaching or administrative position.
- When conducting professional learning classes in the area of technology, it is absolutely crucial that every participant have his or her own computer so that the new skill can be practiced immediately. Simply having a demonstration unit that shows participants what to do is not sufficient. *One learns to do by doing, and doing, and doing!* Therefore, unless the participant practices the skill at least three times during the workshop and is given a follow-up project so that that skill can be practiced many times back in the workplace, new learning is soon forgotten.
- Be certain that a technical support specialist is provided in each school or building to offer direct support and follow-up to teachers who are attempting to acquire new technological knowledge and skill. This specialist should conduct onsite professional learning classes in any new technology deemed necessary for accomplishing local school and/or systemwide goals and provide onsite follow-up and support to faculty and staff members to ensure effective implementation.

REFLECTION AND APPLICATION

> How will I incorporate *technology* into
> professional learning to engage participants' brains?

Which technological activities am I already incorporating into my professional learning?

What additional activities will I incorporate?

Strategy **17**

Visualization and Guided Imagery

WHAT: DEFINING THE STRATEGY

Stephen Covey, author of the *New York Times* bestseller *The 7 Habits of Highly Effective People*, states that everything happens twice, once in the mind and once in reality (Covey, 2004). This is the power of visualization. It is the reason baseball players envision themselves hitting the home run before they come up to bat. It is the reason that Lindsey Vonn, a member of the U.S. Ski team, stood at the top of the hill and envisioned herself skiing down it before she captured the Olympic gold medal. It is the reason that people who accomplish great things see themselves doing so.

It is also the reason that effective school improvement begins with a shared vision. Conzemius and O'Neill (2001) define that vision as an "inspirational picture of the desired future" (p. 26). They further state that a compelling vision has several common features, including the image of a better future for students, staff, and the community, accomplished in a designated time frame, and one that allows school community members to feel that they are contributing to something larger and more positive than the status quo.

Visualization is also a worthwhile strategy to incorporate when teaching adults. Having each teacher see his or her students experiencing success in the classroom during the school year helps to ensure that achievement will be increased. Having teachers imagine their classrooms as reconfigured to be brain compatible helps to make those classrooms active ones! I even visualized each of my books becoming best sellers. As of the writing of this book, I am the author of five best sellers. Remember: *Mind first, reality second!*

WHY: THEORETICAL FRAMEWORK

- Transformation is driven by action. A clear vision gives direction, and actions make movement toward that outcome a reality (Reason & Reason, 2011).
- Both amateur and professional athletes often improve their performance when using mental visual images, which cause the body to line up with their physical success (Lengel & Kuczala, 2010).
- Establishing a vision and executing the action steps necessary to accomplish that vision build momentum toward meaningful transformation (Reason & Reason, 2011).
- Visualization is a powerful strategy for promoting learners' success, since it encourages creativity and supports a state of relaxed alertness (Materna, 2007).
- A focused teacher leader who is a believer that transformational change is possible has the optimism and ability to visualize better outcomes and helps the organization move forward (Reason & Reason, 2011).
- A school's vision includes the belief that every child in the school is capable of achieving at high levels of performance (Danielson, 2009).
- College students who used visual imagery to organize unfamiliar animal information did better than those who used verbal elaboration (Jensen, 2009a).
- Visualization, or seeing in their mind's eyes, is often used by visual learners when they are trying to remember information (Materna, 2007).
- Visionary leaders remind teachers that children are born with intrinsic curiosity and are motivated by the drive to be independent and competent (Danielson, 2009).
- A picture in your mind creates a memory you can find (Sprenger, 2007).
- "All things are created twice. There's a mental or first creation and a physical or second creation to all things" (Covey, 2004, p. 99).

HOW: PROFESSIONAL LEARNING ACTIVITIES

- An effective technique that great presenters use is to visualize themselves successfully presenting to their audience in the room in which they will present prior to the actual presentation. This act alone helps to build confidence and sets presenters' brains in a positive state for the workshop or course.
- New teachers often have the least confidence in their ability to teach and manage students simply because they have the least experience. Have them visualize themselves successfully instructing and managing their classrooms and then facilitate their vision by setting them up for success. In other words, during the first few years, administrators should not give them all of the most challenging students or five or six

different preparations, a floating classroom, or many additional responsibilities until they have had opportunities to experience success. A mentor or peer coach is an essential support for teachers in the beginning years.

- Every teacher should be able to visualize every student in his or her class becoming successful during the school year, even if that student has not been successful before. If teachers cannot see it in their minds, they will not expect it to happen and, therefore, will not afford the child high expectations and treat the child accordingly.

- Have participants in your workshop or course visualize a desired personal goal, such as improving their classroom management or student engagement, and then write a specific plan for accomplishing the visions.

- Representatives from a school's stakeholder groups (such as faculty, staff, parents, students, and community members) should work together to create a shared vision for the school by answering the following question: *What would this school look like if it were the best possible place for teachers to teach and students to learn?* The vision should reflect the achievement of the school's mission and goals and should serve as the barometer by which all decisions are measured. The vision is then shared with as many stakeholders as possible to ascertain feedback. An appropriate vision should motivate all stakeholders both cognitively and affectively.

"I switched from yoga to visualization, for relaxation. I picture a world in which all students with discipline problems attend my class online, from their homes."

- Have participants work individually or in cooperative groups to link a word and its definition by creating visual images. Absurd images result in more vivid visualizations. For example, when teaching the term *hippocampus*, participants are asked to visualize the following: *You are standing on your favorite college campus when you see a herd of hippopotami with mortar boards on their heads strolling single file through a gate.* This visualization links the term *hippocampus* with its definition, *the gateway to long-term memory.*

- Have participants view a vocabulary word, math formula, or science process written on the board or document camera for a few seconds. Then remove the visual and ask participants to visualize the concept and jot it down on their papers. Then have them compare their visualizations with the original.

REFLECTION AND APPLICATION

How will I incorporate *visualization and guided imagery* into professional learning to engage participants' brains?

Which visualization and guided imagery activities am I already incorporating into my professional learning?

What additional activities will I incorporate?

<h1>Strategy 18</h1>

<h1>Visuals</h1>

<h2>WHAT: DEFINING THE STRATEGY</h2>

For many years, I used an overhead projector to show the visuals that accompanied my presentations to adult audiences. I knew that the days of the overhead projector were over several years ago when I requested one at a hotel in which I was presenting. After the I.T. department finished laughing hysterically, they disappeared into a nearby closet and came out several minutes later with a dusty projector. On the top of the overhead was written these words: *This is where dinosaurs go to die!* It was now apparent that this form of technology was outdated and, therefore, I had to make a decision. What technology should I use that would be most appropriate for the way in which I present? For me, PowerPoint was not the answer! I have seen too many adult audiences disengage after looking at PowerPoint slide after slide after slide after slide. What makes it worse is that many presenters read what is on the slide aloud to the audience as if they cannot read for themselves. When I ask adults what is the worst presentation they have ever been a part of as an adult learner, the overwhelming response is *Too many PowerPoint slides and no active engagement!* Look in the How: Professional Learning Activities section of this chapter for some rules of good use of PowerPoint when presenting.

I now use a document camera, which satisfies my visual needs as a presenter. This camera enables me to show my color slides in any order simply by placing them under the projection device. If I read a story, I can show my audience the pictures. If I want them to look at sample student work, they can do that as well. I can even show sample experiments or manipulatives to my entire classes by placing them under the camera. In fact, I am using a document camera that is so portable I am able to transport it in my carry-on luggage. I am very satisfied with my use of visuals and I know that my audience is also. I have had so many people try to *take* my document camera while I am presenting that I now provide them with all of the ordering information so that they can get one of their own.

WHY: THEORETICAL FRAMEWORK

- Humans are intrinsically visual, since the eyes contain about 70% of the sensory receptors of the body and are sending millions of signals each second to the visual processing centers of the brain along the optic nerve (Hyerle & Alper, 2011).
- Incorporating visually related verbs, such as "I see what you mean," into facilitation will help you create rapport with people who are visually dominant (Jensen, 2009b, p. 96).
- Videos enable teachers to look at classrooms in which other teachers are demonstrating new research and processes that they can apply in their own classrooms (Gregory, 2008).
- The brain's ability to change thoughts into images is often seen as a true test of a person's understanding (Hyerle & Alper, 2011).
- Workshop presenters and facilitators who use slides during their presentations should not forget that whatever visuals are being displayed will compete for the attention of the participants (Nash, 2010).
- Visuals often communicate the message or make the point more powerfully than do just words (Allen, 2008a).
- Videos offer teachers a chance to critique the teaching process as they view it and to question why an instructional or assessment process was used (Gregory, 2008).
- The human eyes can take in thirty million pieces of information per second, while the brain can register more than 36,000 images per hour (Jensen, 2007).
- Visual information is highly memorable, since it is fast and easy for the brain to take in (Allen, 2008).
- Visual sources provide 90% of the brain's sensory input (Jensen, 2008).
- The effects of visuals and peripherals increase after about 2 weeks, while the effects of direct instruction diminish during the same time period (Jensen, 2007).

HOW: PROFESSIONAL LEARNING ACTIVITIES

- You are the best visual your audience can have, and believe me, they are watching you! Keep your participants' attention by constantly changing your location in the room so that you are in close proximity to all participants at some point during the professional learning experience. In addition, use gestures and voice tone that show enthusiasm and passion for the content you are teaching. Remember to *teach on your feet, not in your seat!*

- Place visuals on the walls that support the concepts you are teaching. These could include, but are not limited to, posters, a sample agenda, key vocabulary terms, cartoons, and positive messages.

- Design your handouts to be attractive and interactive so that participants are actively engaged in completing them throughout the workshop or course. When educators come into my classes and look at the handouts, they often comment, *There is nothing here!* There is not supposed to be anything there since we fill in the handouts as we go. Just think of the number of times you have attended professional development and received a handout that was so thick that you could sit on it at a football game in order to see better, and that's exactly what you used it for. You never even looked at it after the workshop was over. Let your handouts be a work in progress.

- Incorporate technology into workshops or courses through the use of presentation tools such as Microsoft PowerPoint. Limit the number and frequency of slides, since any tool can be overused. Use the PowerPoint feature to provide participants with a miniature copy of the slides so that attention can be focused on the ensuing discussion. (Refer to *Strategy 16: Technology* for additional suggestions.)

- Design PowerPoint slides according to the following *10-20-30 Guidelines:*

  o Only *10* PowerPoint slides per presentation.
  o No more than *20* minutes in total PowerPoint.
  o Each line on every slide should be at least *30-point* type.

"This PowerPoint slide has a dynamic layout comparing reading scores throughout the district, which you would have seen if I remembered to bring a spare projection bulb."

Allow me to add one more thing. Be sure to intersperse some active engagement such as discussion or reciprocal teaching in with your slides.

- When appropriate, write or draw pertinent concepts and ideas on a flip chart or dry-erase board. Use colored markers to emphasize important points. This will work best when your group is small enough so that no participant has difficulty seeing your visuals.

- Whether your group is small or large, the document camera can work beautifully. Its uses are described in the introductory section of this chapter. I carry my own camera with me so that all schools have to provide is an LCD projector for the camera to be connected to, and I am thoroughly familiar with its operation.

- Utilize symbols, icons, and other concrete images during presentations. For example, when teaching the concept of procedural memory, draw a body to symbolize that anything one learns while the body is engaged is placed in procedural memory, one of the strongest memory systems in the brain.

- Design graphic organizers that are visual representations of linear ideas to use as you present information. These mind maps will assist participants in comprehending the connections between major concepts. (Refer to *Strategy 5: Graphic Organizers, Semantic Maps, and Word Webs* for additional suggestions.)

- Integrate short excerpts or vignettes from television programs or movies that illustrate key concepts into your presentation. These should only last a few minutes. For example, I show a 2-minute excerpt of Ben Stein's classroom in the movie *Ferris Bueller's Day Off* where he is saying *Anyone! Anyone!* to illustrate a classroom in which the teacher is doing all of the talking. He is even answering his own questions. The clip not only makes the point of what a non–brain-compatible classroom looks like, but it is also good for a few laughs.

REFLECTION AND APPLICATION

How will I incorporate *visuals* into
professional learning to engage participants' brains?

Which visuals am I already incorporating into my professional learning?

What additional visuals will I incorporate?

Strategy 19

Work Study, Action Research, and Professional Learning Communities

WHAT: DEFINING THE STRATEGY

I have taught the adult learner for more than 25 years and feel that I have made something of a difference in the way teachers think about engaging students in an effort to increase achievement. I also have more than 300 e-mails from participants in my workshops relating how they have actually increased student achievement as a result of the changes they have made in their teaching practices. However, more times than not, I have left the school with the feeling that, for the majority of teachers, few long-lasting changes in practice would be made solely as a result of attendance at the workshop. Research (Dufour et al., 2010; Joyce & Calhoun, 2010) has proven that I was not mistaken. It has shown that although most teachers understand the concepts being presented in an engaging, well-planned workshop, they seldom change behavior based on the workshop alone. Change comes from job-embedded follow-up and support that can begin with effective preservice and follow-up practices such as internships, on-the-job training, and action research.

121

My daughter, Jennifer, completed her master's degree in education some years ago. At the time, she was teaching third grade. While it would have been so appropriate for her to conduct research with her own students regarding the principles being taught in her classes, that is not what she was required to do. All she did the majority of the time was read books and write papers. What a wasted opportunity to try out some of what she was learning in class in the real-world context of a classroom.

When I am asked to conduct a workshop, I ask the following questions of the administration: (1) How will teachers be provided with support to change their instructional practice if necessary? Remember, it is the behavior that must change first. (2) How will teachers be provided with time to collaborate, discuss, and implement the concepts taught? (3) How will teachers assess changes in student achievement as a result of the implementation of the strategies taught? Sounds a lot like what happens with professional learning communities, doesn't it? We learn to do by doing in authentic contexts. What could be more authentic than the classroom itself?

WHY: THEORETICAL FRAMEWORK

- Teachers who work in grade- or subject-alike professional learning communities (PLCs) have chances to share ideas, strategies, and successful experiences and to find solutions to problems of concern or classroom management dilemmas (Gregory & Herndon, 2010).
- Learning communities that lead to enhanced student learning are those in which teachers collaborate about teaching and learning, increase their expertise through shared knowledge, are driven by the belief that all students can learn, and are focused on classrooms in which students are actively engaged (Lieberman & Miller, 2011).
- High standards must be set and teachers immersed in learning communities that increase the capacity of all teachers and involve them in leading their schools (Duncan, 2011).
- In the world's best-performing school systems, teachers plan lessons jointly, teach those lessons separately, examine the student data, review student work, and then teach the lessons again (Crow, 2009).
- The most effective professional development provides teachers with opportunities to return to their classrooms following the workshop and actually use the strategies taught in an action research setting (Marzano, 2003).
- Our strongest neural networks are created from the actual experiences in which we engage and not from tasks that are not authentic (Westwater & Wolfe, 2000).
- Professional development in Japan incorporates coordinated hands-on efforts to modify teachers' lessons and units within the context of the lesson study (Stigler & Hiebert, 1999).
- Cognitive apprenticeships enable people to acquire not only subject-specific content but also the skills necessary to operate within the content (Berryman & Bailey, 1992).

HOW: PROFESSIONAL LEARNING ACTIVITIES

- As part of a teacher-preparation program, have participants studying to become teachers assigned to the classrooms of master teachers to engage in practicums—specific periods of time during which the observing teacher experiences firsthand the aspects of the teaching profession and may even participate at some level in lesson design and delivery.

- As part of a teacher-preparation program, have participants spend a semester in the classroom of a master teacher serving in the role of a student teacher who experiences the roles and responsibilities of the profession. The student teacher eventually assumes all of the duties of the master teacher during the semester and is evaluated by both the college supervising teacher and the master teacher.

- Following a workshop segment or course of study, have participants implement the knowledge, skills, or strategies learned with their students in their respective classrooms and then return to class and engage in either small-group or whole-class discussion on the effectiveness of the new learning.

- There is no better example of research in action than the PLC. Adhere to the following practices when implementing a successful learning community in your school:

  o Meet regularly and build trusting and open collegial relationships.
  o Develop a clear purpose and focus on challenges during practice.
  o Develop rituals and routines that enable teachers to talk honestly.
  o Have teachers observe, problem solve, support one another, give advice, and teach and learn from one another.
  o Design activities that increase the learning for the students and adults in the building.
  o Have teachers inquire collaboratively and engage in conversations that are informed by student evidence.
  o Have teachers develop a plan of action.
  o Have teachers create the strategies that will connect their personal learning to the learning of students.

Source: Wiedrick, 2011.

- Provide participants who are desirous of becoming adminis-trators the opportunity to shadow an effective veteran administrator. Have the participant follow the administrator and experience a day's events. Following the observation, a discussion ensues regarding the situations observed and the ways in which they were handled.
- Conduct a lesson study by having teachers plan and present a model lesson to their students while other teachers observe the lesson. Following the lesson presentation, have teachers who observed discuss the lesson by asking guiding ques-tions similar to the following:

  o What were the strengths of the lesson?
  o Were the objectives achieved?
  o Cite examples of active student engagement in the lesson.
  o How else could the lesson have been taught?

- Have teachers at a grade level or a department plan a lesson together. Then have each teacher actually teach the lesson to his or her students. Following instruction, have teachers examine student achievement data and review students' work. Based on student outcomes, have them make changes to improve the lesson and then teach it again.

REFLECTION AND APPLICATION

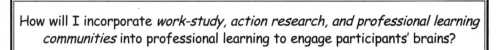

How will I incorporate *work-study, action research, and professional learning communities* into professional learning to engage participants' brains?

Which work-study, action research, and professional learning community activities am I already incorporating into my professional learning?

What additional activities will I incorporate?

Strategy **20**

Writing and Reflection

WHAT: DEFINING THE STRATEGY

A typical staff-development procedure used to be having participants write detailed, voluminous notes as the workshop leader was lecturing. I have even seen participants attempting to copy detailed information from PowerPoint presentations, only to have the presenter move to the next slide when they are only half-way through the copying. You can see the disgusted looks on the faces of the participants. Hopefully those days are over.

We know from brain research that the brain can pay conscious attention to only one thing at a time. Notice I said *conscious* attention. Yes, you can multitask. But only one of those tasks is in your conscious memory simultaneously. The other tasks are unconscious. What, then, does that say about talking on your cell phone while you are driving? One of those two tasks is also unconscious! Text messaging while driving is even worse! But, I digress.

I have a solution that seems to work well when incorporating the brain-compatible strategy of writing into effective instruction. I have participants write words or short phrases either before or after we discuss them or complete graphic organizers together. I write or draw on the screen while they write or draw on their paper. I never ask participants to write and listen simultaneously to me unless I am telling them what to write.

Adult learning theory also tells us that adults need guided opportunities to reflect on new knowledge and competencies

(Jensen, 2008). Journaling affords one of the best methods for such reflection. When participants are given time to write in a reflective journal preceding or following a learning segment, acquisition of knowledge and skill is facilitated. After all, it is not the experience that creates learning, it is the reflection on that experience.

WHY: THEORETICAL FRAMEWORK

- Writing in journals is an effective way to express emotions through a strong and reflective medium (Jensen, 2008).
- Journals and guiding questions focus attention on the topic, provide another tool for monitoring how well people have understood the content, and allow them to freely express their ideas without fear of being ostracized (Algozzine, Campbell, & Wang, 2009).
- People should write about how the content they are learning has application for their personal lives (Jensen, 2008).
- Quick writes help teachers evaluate whether responses are accurate and assist them in clearing up misunderstandings (Jensen & Nickelsen, 2008).
- When learners adopt a note-taking system that is aligned with their learning style, recall can be stimulated by reviewing the notes even after several months have passed (Materna, 2007).
- People should develop a writing vocabulary, spell correctly, learn to organize text, think in hierarchies, and write in a number of different genres (Fogarty, 2009).
- Journals, writer's notebooks, reflections, and diaries take advantage of Gardner's intrapersonal intelligence (Karten, 2007).
- Complicated, multiple bits of information from presentations and observations can be organized and made easier to understand when written down (Jensen, 2000).
- A neurotransmitter called acetylcholine that aids the brain in forming long-term memories is released when neurons connect through speech and through writing (Hannaford, 2005).
- Any group too busy to reflect about its work is too busy to improve (Garmston & Wellman, 1999, p. 63).

HOW: PROFESSIONAL LEARNING ACTIVITIES

- Many presenters give participants voluminous handouts that they will probably never look at again once the professional learning is over. Allow your handouts to be a work in progress. Have participants filling in an incomplete outline, completing a graphic organizer, or writing down short chunks of information to help them remember the major concepts you are teaching. When participants look at some of my handouts, they make the statement, *There's nothing here!* They soon realize that the handout is simply the framework, and by the time the professional learning ends and they have actively written far more than they expected, they also know so much more than they would have if I had supplied all of the information for them ahead of time.

- Have participants write words or short phrases that you wish them to remember either prior to or immediately following your lecture or discussion, or stop and provide time for them to write during it. If participants are attempting to take copious notes while you are talking, they are not free to listen to the subsequent lecture or participate actively in the discussion.

- Stop periodically during a presentation and have participants engage in quick writes. Have them write down in short chunks responses to a question. For example, *Write down three products that students can generate to show you that they have learned the content.* Quick writes take only a minute and can serve to reinforce those things you want your participants to remember.

- If you are going to use PowerPoint slides (and please limit the number you use), then give participants a miniature copy of the PowerPoint or post your PowerPoint presentation to a website where participants know they can access it following the presentation.

- Throughout your course, give participants opportunities to write for a variety of purposes related to the content you are teaching. These purposes could include to persuade, to inform, to express, or to entertain (PIE).

- The following is a great review activity. Give participants a set number of minutes (2 or 3) to write down as many words or phrases as they can remember related to a topic taught in class. Have them compare their list with that of a partner. Each participant gets one point for everything on his or her list that is not on the list of the partner. The object is to accumulate as many points as possible by recalling as much content as possible.

- Here is an adaptation of the aforementioned activity. Give participants a set number of minutes (2 or 3) to write down as many words or phrases as they can recall related to a topic taught in class. Have them compare their list with that of a partner. Anything that their partner has that is accurate that they do not have should be added to their list. The object is to work together to come up with a predetermined number of facts (such as 15) by working cooperatively.

- Give participants various opportunities to show what they have learned through the mode of writing. For example, have them design brochures, newspaper articles, posters, or editorials expressing their opinion on a topic discussed in class.

- Have participants in a leadership class respond in writing to in-basket (real-world) administrative situations by telling how they would handle each one if they were in a school setting. Participants can then share their responses in small groups or with the whole class and discuss how each situation could have been resolved in more than one way.

- At pertinent points during your workshop or course, allow participants to reflect on content by writing in a personal journal. Journals are never graded but provide a meaningful opportunity for participants to apply the content being addressed and their feelings toward it. For example, during a workshop on brain-compatible instructional strategies, participants could write about which strategies they already use consistently with their students and which new ones they would be willing to add to their repertoire.

- Encourage teachers and administrators to write an article for publication in a professional newsletter or journal. This activity enables them to research a topic of interest and receive recognition through the possibility of publication. I never saw myself as a writer until two people—my husband Tyrone and author of the *Differentiated Instruction* series Carolyn Chapman—encouraged me to put my ideas down on paper. The rest is history!

REFLECTION AND APPLICATION

How will I incorporate *writing and reflection*
into professional learning to engage participants' brains?

Which writing and reflection activities am I already incorporating into my professional learning?

What additional activities will I incorporate?

Resource A

Professional Learning Lesson Design

I t is beneficial to see how the 20 professional learning strategies outlined in this book can be incorporated into a lesson plan, whether you are presenting new information in a faculty meeting or workshop or facilitating a yearlong study group in a professional learning community.

A sample lesson plan is displayed on page 140. Each of the six major sections of the plan is described in the paragraphs that follow. The four completed plans following the sample are simply examples of what can happen when the strategies are integrated into a meaningful professional learning experience.

SECTION 1: LESSON OBJECTIVE ■

What is the purpose of this learning opportunity?

During any professional learning opportunity, the first question adults often ask is *Why am I here?* Sometimes they are present not by their own choice but because they have been mandated to be there. Even in times such as these, the situation is improved when the objective of the session is stated. This gives the adult brain purpose. It also keeps the presenter on track during lesson planning. Any teacher of adults will always want to begin with the end in mind (Covey, 2004) by asking the question, *What is the purpose of this learning opportunity?*

■ SECTION 2: SUPPORTING DATA

Why was the objective selected?

The ultimate goal of the professional learning community is to improve the academic achievement of students by improving the knowledge, skills, abilities, and attitudes of the adults who teach them. Therefore, examining student achievement data is essential in determining where the PLC will put its emphasis.

One of Learning Forward's standards for professional learning involves using multiple sources and types of student, educator, and system data to plan, assess, and evaluate professional learning (Learning Forward, 2011). Every meaningful professional development experience should result in increased student achievement. Therefore, every lesson plan should begin with student data that demonstrate the need for the planned experience. This type of thinking eliminates such course offerings as Underwater Basket Weaving or Square Dancing 101. Be certain to include both traditional (norm- or criterion-referenced tests) and authentic (products or performances) assessments in supporting your choice of objectives.

■ SECTION 3: ASSESSMENT

How will you know participants have acquired the knowledge, behavior, or skill?

Waiting until you plan your professional learning and then deciding what your adults should know and be able to do at the end of it is actually too late. The research on assessment says, as soon as you know what you will be teaching, the next question becomes, *How will I know adults have learned the content?*

When I was a student in school, we spent our time trying to guess what the teacher was going to put on the test. If we guessed correctly, we made an A. However, we may have guessed incorrectly and failed even though we studied. We just studied the wrong thing! Determine what knowledge, skills, behaviors, or attitudes you desire adults to have by the end of the professional learning experience and, by all means, tell them! Assessment should not be a well-kept secret.

If adult brains know what you expect, they stand a better chance of meeting your expectations. Here's an analogy. If you are the pilot of a private airplane, how can you plot your route before you know your destination? You can't! You also should not plan your faculty meeting, workshop, or course before you know your destination with adults. That is why the assessment question is the third question of the six and not the sixth and final question.

SECTION 4: WAYS TO GAIN ■ AND MAINTAIN ATTENTION

How will you gain and maintain participants' attention? (Consider need, novelty, meaning, and emotion.)

I have good news and bad news. The bad news is that there are so many stimuli in today's environment that the human brain cannot pay attention to everything at once. Therefore, people can be very selective about what they choose to pay attention to. If a meeting or course is not worthy of attention, then adults' attention is going elsewhere. For example, when I was teaching in Sydney, Australia, a chemistry teacher walked up to me during the first break and pulled a complicated and uncompleted crossword puzzle from his lab jacket. He commented that he had planned to complete the puzzle during the first part of the workshop but, to my credit, he had never thought about the puzzle, since I kept his brain totally engaged. If you do not grab the attention of your adult audience, they will think of other ways to engage their own brains. I have seen adults in workshops making grocery lists, grading papers, talking to peers, texting, and so forth.

Another bit of bad news: There is a structure in the brain called the hippocampus that helps to determine which parts of what you learn will end up in long-term memory. If your content is not deemed important, it stands a slim-to-no chance of getting past the hippocampus. In fact, the hippocampus will hit the delete key at night and your lesson will figuratively end up in the trash. How can you tell if your meeting got deleted? When they come back 24 hours later and you ask them to recall content, it is as if they were not present when you were conducting the initial meeting. Has that ever happened to you? It certainly has to me!

The good news is, if you want to grab adults' attention, hold it throughout your professional learning experience, and keep your content out of the trash, there are four ways to do it. They are need, novelty, meaning, and emotion.

Need

Have you ever learned or remembered something simply because you needed to know it? Here's a true story. Do you remember the plane that landed on the Hudson River? One of the passenger's cell phones was underwater. She needed to call her children and let them know that she was safe, but she had never memorized their numbers nor were they written down any place. Therefore, she could not use the cell phone of another passenger to call her children. I know she now sees the need to memorize those numbers.

Sometimes need will not work with adults. Remember that until adults choose to change their attitude about something, they may not see the need to change their behavior. You may know that they need specific knowledge or a certain skill, but they do not perceive the same need. The good news is that you have three other ways to gain their attention. The second one is novelty.

Novelty

Have you ever noticed that the brain pays attention to things that are new or different in the environment? Things to which we are accustomed become mundane and require little special attention. If adults come to expect that in every faculty meeting, the agenda and content will be the same, they are soon not looking forward to meeting with you after school. As the content changes, so should the strategies.

You may be saying, *But there are only 20 strategies on the entire list*. Where is the novelty in that? Well, think about it. Every one of those 20 strategies has inherent in it endless possibilities for novelty. Think of all the different stories you can tell, the music you can incorporate, or even the projects in which you can engage your adult audience. The possibilities are endless!

Meaning

Adults have often been heard asking this question: *Why do I have to attend this training*? This question indicates adults see no relevance in what is being taught and how it applies to their professional or personal lives. For content to be meaningful, it needs to be connected in some way to adults' lives in the real world. After all, the true purpose of the brain is survival in the real world! Therefore, I am always using real-world examples to make the content I am teaching more meaningful. For example, when teaching about the theory of primacy and recency, which states that the brain remembers what happens first and last in a learning segment more easily than it can remember the middle, I use the real-life example of attorneys taking a great deal of time to prepare opening and closing arguments to sway the jury to rule in their favor. The jury will remember how the case opens and it will remember how the case closes even if it does not recall the testimony of every witness—that is, unless the testimony is emotional, which brings us to the final point.

Emotion

Of all four ways to gain the brain's attention, emotion is probably the most powerful. Why? Emotion places information in one of the strongest memory systems in the brain, reflexive memory. Anything that happened in the world that was emotional, you will not soon forget where you were when it happened. Let's try one. Do you remember where you were when you heard that the *Challenger* space shuttle had exploded and the United States lost seven astronauts? If you were old enough, you probably will remember exactly where you were and what you were doing even though that happened more than 25 years ago!

Yet professional developers do not want to engage adults in negative emotional experiences that are not good for learning. While adults will never forget the experience of being in a negative teacher's class, they will not remember the content acquired during the experience. For example, when I am reading on the plane, as long as the flight is smooth and there is light to moderate turbulence, I can concentrate on the text and comprehend what I am reading. However, several times I have been on flights during which we encountered extreme turbulence. All of a sudden, even if I pretend to be calm and reading, I am reading the same paragraph over and over and, if questioned, would not remember one thing that I am supposedly reading. The ride has become too emotional! My definition of an emotional teacher is one who teaches with enthusiasm and passion and gets adults excited about the topic at hand.

Do not feel compelled to include all four ways—need, novelty, meaning, and emotion—to get the attention of your adult audience in every professional learning experience. If you can effectively incorporate one, that one can lead to a productive session.

■ **SECTION 5: CONTENT CHUNKS AND ACTIVITIES**

How will you structure the learning opportunities to engage adult brains?

Join me in an activity that will help to prove that the brain thinks in connections. Try this with members of your family. Ask them to spell the word shop three times. (s-h-o-p, s-h-o-p, s-h-o-p). Then quickly ask them, *What do you do when you get to a green light*? Nine times out of 10, the answer will be stop, when the correct answer is go. The brain connected or associated the word *light* with the rhyming word *shop*. The closest connection between those two words in many brains is the word *stop*.

When you think about connecting content, remember that the adult brain can only hold between five and nine, or an average of seven, isolated facts in short-term memory simultaneously. This is why so much in life comes in a series of sevens. For example, there are seven days in a week, numbers in a phone number, notes on the scale, colors in the rainbow, seas, continents, habits of highly effective people, initial multiple intelligences, or even dwarfs.

If we are expected to hold more than seven items, then the content needs to be chunked, or connected. This is why a social security number, a telephone number, or a credit card number is in chunks: to make it easier to remember. You see, the brain considers a chunk as one thing rather than as separate things. Therefore, look at your presentation and identify those major chunks that every adult needs to know. For example, in an hour-long faculty meeting, you might incorporate an average of three chunks, since the adult attention span is 20 minutes. Remember to include at least one activity in each chunk you teach. It is the activity that gives the brain time and energy for processing the chunk! Your adult learners will thank you for it!

■ **SECTION 6: PROFESSIONAL LEARNING STRATEGIES**

Which strategies did you incorporate into this plan? How will you support and sustain behavior change?

All 20 of the brain-compatible strategies are listed at the bottom of the lesson plan. This way, teachers will not have to remember them because they will have them listed for ready reference. Even I can't always remember the 20 strategies when I need to do so, and I wrote the book! As you are determining what activities you will include in each chunk of your presentation, you should be incorporating some of the 20 brain-compatible strategies. If you get to the end of your plan and you cannot check off any of the strategies (possibly because your entire inservice consisted of long lectures and PowerPoint, neither of which is brain compatible if overused), go back and plan your inservice again! It is not brain-compatible and will not meet the needs of the majority of your adult learners. Much of it may not even be recalled after a 24-hour period.

I have often been asked, *How many strategies should I incorporate in one lesson, or one chunk?* There is no magic number. Using too many strategies at one time can be just as detrimental as using too few. A rule of thumb I try to teach by is as follows: Make sure that at some point during the professional learning experience, you have incorporated at least one visual, one auditory, one tactile, and one kinesthetic strategy, since you will have adults with all four modality preferences in your audience. That doesn't mean one strategy of each modality per chunk, but one strategy of each modality per session.

CRUCIAL QUESTIONS ■

In summary, every professional developer should ask and answer the following questions during the planning process:

1. What is the purpose of this learning opportunity? What data support the selection of this purpose?

2. How will I know that participants have acquired the knowledge, behavior, or skill? How will I know that student achievement has increased?

3. How will I gain and maintain participants' attention? (*Consider need, novelty, meaning, and emotion.*)

4. How will I structure the learning into segments? Which activities will I integrate into each segment to engage adult brains?

5. Which of the 20 professional learning strategies did I incorporate into my lesson plans?

6. How can I celebrate the success of this professional learning experience?

PROFESSIONAL LEARNING LESSON PLAN
Sample Plan

Lesson Objective(s): *What is the purpose of this learning opportunity?*

Supporting Data: *Why was the objective selected?*

Assessment: *How will you know participants have acquired the knowledge, behavior, or skill? How will you know the objective was achieved?*

Ways to Gain/Maintain Attention (Primacy): *How will you gain and maintain participants' attention? Consider need, novelty, meaning, and emotion.*

Content Chunks and Activities: *How will you structure the learning opportunities to engage adult brains?*

Lesson Segment 1:

Activities:

Lesson Segment 2:

Activities:

Lesson Segment 3:

Activities:

Professional Learning Strategies: *Which strategies did you incorporate into this plan? How will you support and sustain behavior change?*

- ☐ Brainstorming/Discussion
- ☐ Drawing/Artwork
- ☐ Field Trips
- ☐ Games
- ☐ Graphic Organizers
- ☐ Humor/Celebration
- ☐ Manipulatives/Models
- ☐ Metaphors/Analogies/Similes
- ☐ Mnemonic Devices
- ☐ Movement
- ☐ Music/Rhythm/Rhyme/Rap
- ☐ Project/Problem-Based Instruction
- ☐ Reciprocal Teaching/Cooperative Learning/Peer Coaching
- ☐ Role Play/Drama/ Pantomime/Charades
- ☐ Storytelling
- ☐ Technology
- ☐ Visualization
- ☐ Visuals
- ☐ Work Study/Action Research
- ☐ Writing/Reflection

Resource B

Sample Professional Learning Lesson Designs

Classroom Management (Series of Workshops)

Lesson Objective(s): *What is the purpose of this learning opportunity?*

To decrease the number of disciplinary infractions and office referrals.

Supporting Data: *Why was the objective selected?*

Twenty percent of the student body has been referred to the office at least once annually.

Assessment: *How will you know participants have acquired the knowledge, behavior, or skill? How will you know the objective was achieved?*

Teachers will observe one another for the practices taught. Disciplinary infractions will decrease by 50%.

Ways to Gain/Maintain Attention (Primacy): *How will you gain and maintain participants' attention? Consider need, novelty, meaning, and emotion.*

Teachers brainstorm/discuss reasons why some of today's students can be more difficult to manage and teach than students in the past.

Content Chunks and Activities: *How will you structure the learning opportunities to engage adult brains?*

Lesson Segment 1: Teachers learn to create a physical environment conducive to learning.

Activities: Mini-lecture on the effects of color, music, lighting, aroma, and seating while teachers complete graphic organizer. Teachers walk around the room to high-energy music, stop, and review content just learned. Teachers reflect on how they can change the physical environment in their classrooms in light of information gleaned.

Lesson Segment 2: Teachers learn to establish rules, rituals, and responsibility.

Activities: Teachers bring a list of established rules, expectations, and procedures for their classroom and share ones that are working well with cooperative group. Teachers share ideas and take notes from mini-lecture on rituals and procedures. Teachers put together a proactive plan for students and begin implementing it.

Lesson Segment 3: Teachers learn strategies for dealing with chronic behavior disorders.

Activities: Teachers read *Different Brains, Different Learners* by Eric Jensen (2010) to learn ways to deal with the most challenging students. They select one challenging student as a case study and apply some of the techniques learned. Share with a partner. Observe partner twice in classroom setting using practices learned.

Professional Learning Strategies: *Which strategies did you incorporate into this plan? How will you support and sustain behavior change?*

- ☑ Brainstorming/Discussion
- ☐ Drawing/Artwork
- ☐ Field Trips
- ☐ Games
- ☑ Graphic Organizers
- ☑ Humor/Celebration
- ☐ Manipulatives/Models
- ☐ Metaphors/Analogies/Similes
- ☐ Mnemonic Devices
- ☑ Movement
- ☑ Music/Rhythm/Rhyme/Rap
- ☑ Project/Problem-Based Instruction
- ☑ Reciprocal Teaching/Cooperative Learning/Peer Coaching
- ☐ Role Play/Drama/Pantomime/Charades
- ☑ Storytelling
- ☐ Technology
- ☐ Visualization
- ☑ Visuals
- ☐ Work Study/Action Research
- ☑ Writing/Reflection

Partners will observe one another periodically throughout the year. Administrators will observe teachers citing improved classroom management and providing any necessary continued support.

Peer Coaching:
Ongoing Throughout the School Year

Lesson Objective(s): *What is the purpose of this learning opportunity?*

To decrease the teacher turnover rate by retaining beginning teachers in the profession.

Supporting Data: *Why was the objective selected?*

The teacher turnover rate in the building has been higher than 25% for 3 consecutive years.

Assessment: *How will you know participants have acquired the knowledge, behavior, or skill? How will you know the objective was achieved?*

Beginning teachers will increase student achievement and remain on staff, decreasing attrition rate to a maximum of 10%.

Ways to Gain/Maintain Attention (Primacy): *How will you gain and maintain participants' attention? Consider need, novelty, meaning, and emotion.*

New teachers will be welcomed and celebrated. Data will be shared with beginning teachers and their coaches regarding the considerable value that coaches play in supporting and retaining beginning teachers.

Content Chunks and Activities: *How will you structure the learning opportunities to engage adult brains?*

Lesson Segment 1: Beginning teachers and trained coaches get acquainted.

Activities: Beginning teachers and trained coaches meet at an after-school get-acquainted activity. Play Facts in Four game to get to know one another (Refer to *Strategy 4: Games* for directions).

Lesson Segment 2: Mutually agreed-upon goals for improving instruction are set.

Activities: Coaches observe beginning teachers at a mutually agreed-upon time to look for strengths and areas for improvement. Coaches and teachers discuss the observation and set short-term goals together.

Lesson Segment 3: Observations and meetings indicate progress.

Activities: Beginning teachers and coaches observe one another in light of the mutually agreed-upon goals and meet regularly to discuss progress.

Lesson Segment 4: Teachers and coaches celebrate success.

Activities: At the end of the year, teachers and coaches celebrate success by reflecting on goals achieved and improvements in student achievement throughout the year.

Professional Learning Strategies: *Which strategies did you incorporate into this plan? How will you support and sustain behavior change?*

☑ Brainstorming/Discussion
☐ Drawing/Artwork
☐ Field Trips
☑ Games
☐ Graphic Organizers
☑ Humor/Celebration
☐ Manipulatives/Models
☐ Metaphors/Analogies/Similes
☐ Mnemonic Devices
☐ Movement
☐ Music/Rhythm/Rhyme/Rap
☐ Project/Problem-Based Instruction

☑ Reciprocal Teaching/Cooperative Learning/Peer Coaching
☐ Role Play/Drama/Pantomime/Charades
☐ Storytelling
☐ Technology
☐ Visualization
☐ Visuals
☐ Work Study/Action Research
☑ Writing/Reflection

Peer coaches will support beginning teachers throughout the year in the setting and attainment of goals.

School-Improvement Planning Workshop–Part I

Lesson Objective(s): *What is the purpose of this learning opportunity?*

To develop a vision statement for Lanier High School.

Supporting Data: *Why was this objective selected?*

All stakeholders need a collaborative view of what students should know and be able to do when they leave this school.

Assessment: *How will you know participants have acquired the knowledge, behavior, or skill?*

A vision statement will be developed that 70% of stakeholders support.

How will you know the objective was achieved?

Teachers will measure current student performance in light of the vision statement.

Ways to Gain/Maintain Attention (Primacy): *How will you gain and maintain participants' attention?*

Participants close their eyes and envision Lanier High School as a place where all students can achieve. They discuss their visions.

Content Chunks and Activities: *How will you structure the learning opportunities to engage adult brains?*

Lesson Segment 1: Stakeholders develop vision statement.

Activities: Participants work in cooperative groups to complete the following "dream activity." For Lanier High School to be a place where all students can achieve, what would it look like? A spokesperson for each group reports, the facilitator combines like ideas, and consensus of vision is reached. Participants close their eyes again and envision the fulfillment of their vision statement. The faculty celebrates.

Follow-Up and Implementation Strategies: *How will you support and sustain behavior change?*

The vision statement is posted and kept at the forefront of every endeavor.

Professional Learning Strategies

Which strategies did you incorporate into this plan?

☑ Brainstorming/Discussion
☐ Drawing/Artwork
☐ Field Trips
☐ Games
☐ Graphic Organizers
☑ Humor/Celebration
☐ Manipulatives/Models
☐ Metaphors/Analogies/Similes
☐ Mnemonic Devices
☐ Movement
☐ Music/Rhythm/Rhyme/Rap
☐ Project/Problem-Based Instruction

☑ Reciprocal Teaching/Cooperative Learning/Peer Coaching
☐ Role Play/Drama/Pantomime/Charades
☐ Storytelling
☐ Technology
☑ Visualization
☐ Visuals
☐ Work Study/Action Research
☑ Writing/Reflection

The vision statement will serve as the focal point for all instructional decision-making.

School-Improvement Planning
Workshop–Part II

Lesson Objective(s): *What is the purpose of this learning opportunity?*

To examine student achievement data in light of the developed vision.

Supporting Data: *Why was the objective selected?*

Stakeholders need to discern the discrepancy between the desired vision and current student achievement data.

Assessment: *How will you know participants have acquired the knowledge, behavior, or skill? How will you know the objective was achieved?*

Teachers will address priorities during instruction. Student achievement in identified areas increases.

Ways to Gain/Maintain Attention (Primacy): *How will you gain and maintain participants' attention? Consider need, novelty, meaning, and emotion.*

Stakeholders will review the vision statement, visualize it, and create a slogan that exemplifies its content.

Content Chunks and Activities: *How will you structure the learning opportunities to engage adult brains?*

Lesson Segment 1: Stakeholders meet in grade-level/departmental groups to examine norm- and criterion-referenced data and samples of student work to determine areas of student strengths and improvement needs.

Activities: Discuss data and pinpoint priorities for instruction. Share priorities with total group and look for patterns across grade levels/departments. Post identified areas on wall. Have group leaders place dots next to common priorities.

Lesson Segment 2: Groups determine when and how priorities will be addressed in daily lessons.

Activities: Stakeholders discuss priorities and plan lessons incorporating skills and strategies for instruction.

Professional Learning Strategies: *Which strategies did you incorporate into this plan? How will you support and sustain behavior change?*

- ☑ Brainstorming/Discussion
- ☐ Drawing/Artwork
- ☐ Field Trips
- ☐ Games
- ☐ Graphic Organizers
- ☐ Humor/Celebration
- ☑ Manipulatives/Models
- ☐ Metaphors/Analogies/Similes
- ☐ Mnemonic Devices
- ☑ Movement
- ☐ Music/Rhythm/Rhyme/Rap
- ☐ Project/Problem-Based Instruction

- ☑ Reciprocal Teaching/Cooperative Learning/Peer Coaching
- ☐ Role Play/Drama/Pantomime/Charades
- ☐ Storytelling
- ☐ Technology
- ☑ Visualization
- ☑ Visuals
- ☐ Work Study/Action Research
- ☑ Writing/Reflection

Administrators and coaches monitor lesson plans for inclusion of priorities. Administrators look for priorities during classroom observations.

Resource C

Tips for Making Your Professional Learning Unforgettable

1. Arrive early so that you can set up before participants arrive. Get to your training location at least 45 minutes prior to the time the workshop is scheduled to begin. You can't greet your participants if you are getting ready for your meeting or course.

2. Greet your participants at the door, shake their hands, and welcome them to your presentation. Even adult students learn more from teachers they like than from those they don't. Begin your relationship with your participants at your classroom door.

3. Have calming (or high-energy) music playing when your participants arrive depending on what state you want to create in their brains. You can change the state of your participants' brains with the type of music you play. Calm them or invigorate them with your choice of music.

4. Start your workshop on time even if all participants are not present. Honor those who have come on time by starting on time! If you don't, the next time, those who came on time will not see the need to repeat that behavior.

5. Know your content. You can't teach what you don't know! You can't add the sparkles (music, jokes, cartoons, stories) if you are not confident in the content you are teaching.

6. Don't be a *know-it-all*! Your participants have vast amounts of knowledge that they should be given opportunities to exhibit. You don't have all the answers. You can learn as much from your participants as they are learning from you. Allow them to share.

7. Establish a purpose for your professional learning opportunity. *Begin with the End in Mind* (Covey, 2004). If participants don't know the purpose of your meeting, workshop, or course, how will they know when they have accomplished it?

8. Open in a memorable way. Since the brain remembers best what it hears first, make your opening unforgettable. Tell an emotional story, use a role play, or play moving music to make your learning experience meaningful.

9. Establish your rituals and procedures for ensuring that the activities proceed smoothly. Chaos is not brain compatible! Be sure that you teach your participants your rituals and expectations so that active engagement will be easy to implement. They need to know when to talk to one another and when to move.

10. Divide your presentation into chunks or segments and include some type of activity in each segment. The adult brain can only hold an average of seven bits of information in short-term memory simultaneously, and the average attention span is about 20 minutes. Take your one-hour faculty meeting and divide it into three chunks. Be sure to put some activity in each chunk.

11. Integrate the 20 brain-compatible strategies into your professional learning opportunity. Be sure you have included strategies for your visual, auditory, tactile, and kinesthetic leaners. They will all thank you!

12. Give participants an incentive, such as a joke, for returning from breaks and lunch on time. Participants will want to hurry back from breaks and lunch when they know that you will be showing a humorous cartoon or telling a hilarious joke. Tell your best joke following lunch.

13. Use music to bring participants back from breaks and lunch. Pick an appropriate song and tell participants that by the time it ends, they must be settled in their seats. Then watch them do it without you having to say a word.

14. Stop and summarize content throughout the presentation. Most brains need to hear something at least three times before it even begins to stick. Don't wait to the end of your meeting to summarize. Do it at the end of each learning segment or chunk.

15. Provide time for reflection on an activity by having participants talk together or write in a reflection journal. Remember it

is not the activity that is important. It is the reflection regarding the activity that makes the difference.

16. Interject humor throughout your presentation with appropriate jokes, riddles, and/or cartoons. You can serve the role of *class clown* on the first day of class. Then have a participant volunteer to tell the jokes on subsequent days. You would be surprised how hilarious some teachers can be when given the opportunity.

17. Incorporate stories that will reinforce the points you are making. Stories enable the brain to relax and digest the content you are teaching. When people remember your story, they remember the point you were making by telling it.

18. Close in a memorable way. The brain remembers second best what it hears last in a learning segment. Make sure their last memory of you is unforgettable!

19. End on time or slightly ahead of time and leave them wanting more! When your workshop is over and your participants ask *Is it time to go already?* you will know that you have scored a winning performance.

20. Determine what follow-up or support will be needed for participants to implement what was learned in the professional learning experience. Will there be a follow-up project? Will teachers need a peer coach to support them through the behavior change? Which actions stand the best chance of guaranteeing success?

Resource D

Secrets for Looking Younger, Staying Healthier, and Living Longer

One of the side benefits of attending any of my classes is that I not only provide information that will help participants professionally to become better teachers or administrators, I also supply them with concepts that will help them personally to become better individuals. After all, the better person you are, the better teacher you become! What we know from the research on androgyny and the study of the brain is that certain practices appear to enable people to look 5 to 10 years younger than their age, stay healthier than most other people, and live a longer, productive life. Many of those practices have been mentioned in the pages of this book. However, in case you did not locate them, here are the 10 things that keep people living above the age of 80 according to the American Association of Retired Persons (Mahoney, 2005):

1. **Heredity**—If your parents lived longer, you stand a better chance of living longer.

2. **Purpose**—People who have a specific reason to get up in the morning and stay active live longer.

3. **Close personal relationships**—People who are around other human beings (and pets, by the way) live longer.

4. **Humor**—People who laugh a lot (even fake laughter) strengthen their immunity and live longer.

5. **Optimism**—People who look at the positive side of life or see the glass as *half-full rather than half-empty* live longer.

6. **Exercise**—People who keep their bodies engaged through physical activity, (i.e., aerobics, walking, swimming, skiing, yoga, and so forth) live longer.

7. **A job you are passionate about**—*"If you love your job, you will never work a day in your life."* Your job will be play, not work, and you will live longer.

8. **Music**—People who learn to play a musical instrument or enjoy the powerful, positive effects of music live longer.

9. **Games**—You don't stop playing games because you grow old; you grow old because you stop playing games. Play and live longer.

10. **Spirituality**—People who believe in a higher power outside of themselves live longer.

Source: Tate, 2011

Heredity does not work for me or my mother. My father died at age 58 and my mother lost 10 brothers and sisters before the age of 72. However, we practice the other nine concepts, and they appear to be working for us. I just celebrated my sixth decade of life, and my mother is nearing 90. In fact, I am having so much fun teaching the adult brain that I plan to live forever! Please join me!

Bibliography

Algozzine, B., Campbell, P., & Wang, A. (2009). *63 tactics for teaching diverse learners: Grades 6–12*. Thousand Oaks, CA: Corwin.

Allen, R. (2008a). *Green light classrooms: Teaching techniques that accelerate learning*. Victoria, Australia: Hawker Brownlow.

Allen, R. (2008b). *The ultimate book of music for learning*. Victoria, Australia: Hawker Brownlow.

Anderson, L. W., & Krathwohl, D. R. (2001). *A taxonomy for learning, teaching, and assessing*. New York: Addison Wesley Longman.

Armstrong, T. (1994). *Multiple intelligences in the classroom*. Alexandria, VA: Association for Supervision and Curriculum Development.

Baumgarten, S. (2006, July). Meaningful movement for children: Stay true to their natures. *Teaching Elementary Physical Education*, 9–11.

Berryman, S. E., & Bailey, T. R. (1992). *The double helix of education and the economy*. New York: Institute on Education and the Economy, Columbia University Teachers College.

Bloom, B. S. (Ed.). (1956). *Taxonomy of educational objectives. The classification of educational goals, by a committee of college and university examiners*. New York: Longmans.

Brown, J. S. (2008). How to connect technology and passion in the service of learning. *Chronicle of Higher Education, 55*(8), A99.

Burgess, R. (2000). *Laughing lessons: 149 2/3 ways to make teaching and learning fun*. Minneapolis, MN: Free Spirit Publishing.

Burns, M., Menchaca, M., & Dimock, V. (2001). *Applying technology to restructuring and learning*. Paper presented at 2002 Computer Support for Collaborative Larning (CSCL) Conference. Pedagogy Track: Teachers and CSCI, Boulder, CO.

Buzan, T. (1993). *The mind map book*. New York: Dutton.

Caine, R. N., Caine, G., McClintic, C., & Klimek, K. J. (2009). *12 brain/mind learning principles in action: Developing executive functions of the human brain*. Thousand Oaks, CA: Corwin.

Carroll, T. (2009). The next generation of learning teams. *Phi Delta Kappan, 91*(2), 8–13.

Chenoweth, K. (2009). It can be done, it's being done, and here's how. *Phi Delta Kappan, 91*(1), 38–43.

Collins, D. (2000). *Achieving your vision of professional development: How to assess your needs and get what you want*. Tallahassee, FL: SERVE.

Conzemius, A., & O'Neill, J. (2001). *Building shared responsibility for student learning.* Alexandria, VA: Association for Supervision and Curriculum Development.

Cookson, P.W. (2001, September). The online professional seminar: E-learning may aid professional development but there's no virtual miracle in sight. *Education Week.*

Costa, A. L. (2008). *School as a home for the mind: Creating mindful curriculum, instruction, and dialogue.* Victoria, Australia: Hawker Brownlow.

Covey, S. R. (2004). *The 7 habits of highly effective people: Powerful lessons in personal change.* New York: Free Press.

Crow, T. (Winter, 2009). What works, works everywhere. (Q & A: Michael Barber). *Journal of the National Staff Development Council, 30*(1), 10–16.

Danielson, C. (2009). *Talk about teaching! Leading professional conversations.* Thousand Oaks, CA: Corwin.

Darling-Hammond, L., Wei, R. C., Andree, A., Richardson, N., & Orphanos, S. (2009). *Professional learning in the learning profession: A status report on teacher development in the United States and abroad.* Dallas, TX: National Staff Development Council.

Delandtsheer, J. (2011). *Making all kids smarter: Strategies that help all students reach their highest potential.* Thousand Oaks, CA: Corwin.

Delehant, A. M. (2007). *Making meetings work: How to get started, get going, and get it done.* Thousand Oaks, CA: Corwin.

Deutschman, C. S. (2005). Transcription. *Critical Care Medicine, 33*(Suppl.), S400–S403.

Dewey, J. (1934). *Art as experience.* New York: Minion Ballet.

Duncan, A. (2011). Forge a commitment to authentic professional learning. *Learning Forward Journal, 32*(4), 70–72.

Dufour, R. P. (1991). *The principal as staff developer.* Bloomington, IN: National Educational Service.

Dufour, R., Dufour, R., Eaker, R., & Many, T. (2010). *Learning by doing: A handbook for professional learning communities at work.* Bloomington, IN: Solution Tree Press.

Edwards, B. (1999). *The new drawing on the right side of the brain.* New York: Tarcher/Putnam.

Feinstein, S. G. (2009). *Secrets of the teenage brain: Research-based strategies for reaching and teaching today's adolescents* (2nd ed.). Thousand Oaks, CA: Corwin.

Feinstein, S. G., & Kiner, R. W. (2011). *The brain and strengths-based school leadership.* Thousand Oaks, CA: Corwin.

Fogarty, R. (2001). *Making sense of the research on the brain and learning.* Victoria, Australia: Hawker Brownlow.

Fogarty, R. (2009). *Brain-compatible classrooms* (3rd ed.). Victoria, Australia: Hawker Brownlow.

Gardner, H. (1983). *Frames of mind: The theory of multiple intelligences.* New York: Basic Books.

Gardner, H. (1999). *Intelligence reframed: Multiple intelligences for the 21st century.* New York: Basic Books.

Garmston, R., & Wellman, B. (1999). *The adaptive school: A sourcebook for developing collaborative groups.* Norwood, MA: Christopher-Gordon.

Ginsberg, M. B. (2011). *Transformative professional learning: A system to enhance teacher and student motivation.* Thousand Oaks, CA: Corwin.

Glasser, W. (1990). *The quality school: Managing students without coercion.* New York: HarperCollins.

Goodlad, J. (1984). *A place called school.* New York: McGraw-Hill.

Gregory, G. H. (2008). *Differentiated instructional strategies in practice: Training, implementation, and supervision.* Thousand Oaks, CA: Corwin.

Gregory, G. H., & Herndon, L. E. (2010). *Differentiated instructional strategies for the block schedule.* Thousand Oaks, CA: Corwin.

Gregory, G. H., & Kuzmich, L. (2007). *Teacher teams that get results: 61 strategies for sustaining and renewing professional learning communities.* Thousand Oaks, CA: Corwin.

Gregory, G. H., & Parry, T. (2006). *Designing brain-compatible learning* (3rd ed.). Thousand Oaks, CA: Corwin.

Guskey, T. R. (1999). *Evaluating professional development.* Thousand Oaks, CA: Corwin.

Hannaford, C. (2005). *Smart moves: Why learning is not all in your head.* Arlington, VA: Great River Books.

Hord, S. (2009). Professional learning communities. *Journal of the National Staff Development Council, 30*(1), 40–43.

Hyerle, D. N., & Alper, L. (2011). *Student successes with thinking maps: School-based research, results, and models for achievement using visual tools* (2nd ed.). Thousand Oaks, CA: Corwin.

Jensen, E. (2000). Moving with the brain in mind. *Educational Leadership, 58*(3), 34–37.

Jensen, E. (2001). *Arts with the brain in mind.* Alexandria, VA: Association for Supervision and Curriculum Development.

Jensen, E. (2005). *Top tunes for teaching: 977 song titles and practical tools for choosing the right music every time.* Thousand Oaks, CA: Corwin.

Jensen, E. (2007). *Brain-compatible strategies* (2nd ed.). Victoria, Australia: Hawker Brownlow.

Jensen, E. (2008). *Brain-based learning: The new paradigm of teaching.* Thousand Oaks, CA: Corwin.

Jensen, E. (2009a). *Fierce teaching: Purpose, passion and what matters most.* Thousand Oaks, CA: Corwin.

Jensen, E. (2009b). *Super teaching* (4th ed.). Victoria, Australia: Hawker Education.

Jensen, E. (2010). *Different brains, different learners: How to reach the hard to reach* (2nd ed.). Thousand Oaks, CA: Corwin.

Jensen, E., & Dabney, M. (2000). *Learning smarter: The new science of teaching.* San Diego, CA: The Brain Store.

Jensen, E., & Nickelsen, L. (2008). *Deeper learning: 7 powerful strategies for in-depth and longer-lasting learning.* Victoria, Australia: Hawker Brownlow.

Jones, C. (2008). *The magic of metaphor.* Retrieved October 23, 2011, from http://www.uxmatters.com/mt/archives/2008/10/the-magic-of-metaphor.php.

Jonson, K. F. (2002). *Being an effective mentor: How to help beginning teachers succeed.* Thousand Oaks, CA: Corwin.

Joyce, B., & Calhoun, E. (2010). *Models of professional development: A celebration of educators.* Thousand Oaks, CA: Corwin.

Karten, T. J. (2007). *More inclusion strategies that work!* Victoria, Australia: Hawker Brownlow.

Keeley, P. (2008). *Science formative assessment: 75 practical strategies for linking assessment, instruction, and learning.* Thousand Oaks, CA: Corwin & National Science Teachers Association.

Khalsa, D. S. (1997). *Brain longevity: The breakthrough medical program that improves your mind and memory.* New York: Warner Books.

Killion, J. (2009). Coaches' roles, responsibilities, and reach. In J. Knight, *Coaching approaches and perspectives* (pp. 7–28). Thousand Oaks, CA: Corwin.

Kluger, J. (2005, January 17). The funny thing about laughter. *Time. 165*(3), A24–A29.

Knight, J. (2009). *Coaching: Approaches and perspectives.* Thousand Oaks, CA: Corwin.

Krepel, W. J., & Duvall, C. R. (1981). *Field trips: A guide for planning and conducting educational experiences.* Washington, DC: National Education Association.

Learning Forward. (2011). *Standards for professional learning.* Retrieved December 29, 20122, from www.learningforward.org/standards/standards.cfm.

Lakoff, G., & Johnson, M. (2011). *Metaphors we live by.* Chicago: University of Chicago Press.

Lemmon, K. (2008). Prepared for the worst. *School planning & management.* Retrieved November 9, 2011, from www.peterli.com/spm/resources/articles/archive.php?article_id=1965.

Lengel, T., & Kuczala, M. (2010). *The kinesthetic classroom: Teaching and learning through movement.* Thousand Oaks, CA: Corwin.

Lieberman, A., & Miller, L. (2011, August). Learning communities: The starting point for professional learning is in schools and classrooms. *Journal of Staff Development, 32*(4), 16–17, 19–20.

Mahoney, S. (2005, July/August). How to live longer. *American Association of Retired People, 48*(4B), 64–72.

Markowitz, K., & Jensen, E. (2007). *The great memory book.* Victoria, Australia: Hawker Brownlow.

Marzano, R. J. (2003). *What works in schools: Translating research into action.* Alexandria, VA: Association for Supervision and Curriculum Development.

Marzano, R. J. (2007). *The art and science of teaching: A comprehensive framework for effective instruction.* Victoria, Australia: Hawker Brownlow.

Materna, L. (2007). *Jump start the adult learner: How to engage and motivate adults using brain-compatible strategies.* Thousand Oaks, CA: Corwin.

McCarthy, B. (1990). Using the 4MAT system to bring learning styles to schools. *Educational Leadership, 48*(2), 31–37.

Medina, J. (2008). *Brain rules: 12 principles for surviving and thriving at work, home, and school.* Seattle, WA: Pear Press.

Mezirow, J. (1991). *Transformative dimensions of adult learning.* San Francisco: Jossey-Bass.

Nash, R. (2010). *The active workshop: Practical strategies for facilitating professional learning.* Thousand Oaks, CA: Corwin.

National Governors Association Center for Best Practices, Council of Chief State School Officers. (2010). Common core state standards. Washington, DC: National Governors Association Center for Best Practices, Council of Chief State School Officers. Retrieved from http://www.corestandards .org

National Staff Development Council. (2006). *Collaboration skills.* Accessed July 12, 2011, at www.nsdc.org/standards/collaborationskills.cfm.

Nolly, G. (2011, August). 4 components critical to principal development. *Journal of Staff Development, 32*(4), 64–68.

Paben, (2002). What's in it for the busy leader? *Journal of Staff Development, 23*(1), 22–27.

Patterson, K., Grenny, J., Maxfield, D., McMillan, R., & Switzler, A. (2008). *Influencer: The power to change anything.* New York: McGraw-Hill.

Perez, K. (2008*). More than 100 brain-friendly tools and strategies for litereacy instruction.* Thousand Oaks, CA: Corwin.

Pitler, H., Hubbell, E. R., Kuhn, M., & Malenoski, K. (2007). *Using technology with classroom instruction that works.* Alexandria, VA: Association for Supervision and Curriculum Development.

Ratey, J. (2008). *SPARK: The revolutionary new science of exercise and the brain.* New York: Little, Brown and Company.

Reason, C., & Reason, C. (2011). *Mirror images: New reflections on teacher leadership.* Thousand Oaks, CA: Corwin.

Ronis, D. L. (2006). *Brain-compatible mathematics* (2nd ed.). Thousand Oaks, CA: Corwin.

Sebesta, L. M., & Martin, S. R. M. (2004). Fractions: Building a foundation with concrete manipulatives. *Illinois Schools Journal, 83*(2), 3–23.

Senge, P. (1990). *The fifth discipline: The art and practice of the learning organization.* New York: Doubleday.

Sergiovanni, T. J. (1992). *Moral leadership: Getting to the heart of school improvement.* San Francisco: Jossey-Bass.

Silberman, M. (1999). *101 ways to make meetings active: Surefire ways to engage your group.* San Francisco: Jossey-Bass/Pfeiffer.

Snyder, K. J. (2005). Competency development: Linking restructuring goals to training and coaching. In R. Anderson & K. Snyder (Eds.), *Clinical supervision: Coaching for higher performance.* Lancaster, PA: Technomics.

Sousa, D. A. (2001). *How the brain learns* (2nd ed.). Thousand Oaks, CA: Corwin.

Sousa, D. A. (2006). *How the brain learns* (3rd ed.) Thousand Oaks, CA: Corwin.

Sparks, D. (2009, Winter). Reach for the heart as well as the mind. *Journal of the National Staff Development Council, 30*(1), 48–54.

Sprenger, M. (2007). *Memory 101 for educators.* Thousand Oaks, CA: Corwin.

Sternberg, R. J. (1997). *Successful intelligence: How practical and creative intelligence determine success in life.* New York: First Plume.

Sternberg, R. J., & Grigorenko, E. L. (2000). *Teaching for successful intelligence. To increase student learning and achievement.* Arlington Heights, IL: Skylight.

Stigler, J. W., & Hiebert, J. (1999). *The teaching gap: Best ideas from the world's teachers for improving education in the classroom.* New York: Free Press.

Summerford, L. (2000). *PE for me.* Champaign, IL: Human Kinetics.

Sylwester, R. (2010). *A child's brain: The need for nurture.* Thousand Oaks, CA: Corwin.

Tanner, M. L., & Cassados, L. (1998). Writing to learn. In J. Irwin & M. Doyle (Eds.), *Reading/writing connections: Learning from research* (pp. 145–159). Newark, DE: International Reading Association.

Tate, M. L. (2010). *Worksheets don't grow dendrites: 20 instructional strategies that engage the brain.* Thousand Oaks, CA: Corwin.

Tate, M. L. (2011). *Preparing children for success in school and in life: 20 ways to increase your child's brain power.* Thousand Oaks, CA: Corwin.

Tileston, D. W. (2011). *10 best teaching practices: How brain research and learning styles define teaching competencies* (3rd ed.). Thousand Oaks, CA: Corwin.

Underwood, A. (2005, October 3). The good heart. *Newsweek,* 48–55.

University of California–Los Angeles. (2009, October 19). First-time Internet users find boost in brain function after just one week. *ScienceDaily.* Retrieved from www.sciencedaily.com/releases/2009/10/091019134707htm.

Westwater, A., & Wolfe, P. (2000). The brain-compatible curriculum. *Educational Leadership, 58*(3), 49–52.

Weinberger, N. M. (2004). Music and the brain. *Scientific American, 291*(5), 88–95.

Wiedrick, J. (2011, August). We're all in this together. *Journal of Staff Development, 32*(4), 19.

Wilson, F. (1999). *The hand: How its use shapes the brain, language, and human culture.* New York: Vintage Books.

Wolfe, P. (2001). *Brain matters: Translating research into classroom practice.* Alexandria, VA: Association for Supervision and Curriculum Development.

Index

CORWIN
A SAGE Company

The Corwin logo—a raven striding across an open book—represents the union of courage and learning. Corwin is committed to improving education for all learners by publishing books and other professional development resources for those serving the field of PreK–12 education. By providing practical, hands-on materials, Corwin continues to carry out the promise of its motto: **"Helping Educators Do Their Work Better."**